On the Bright Side

On the Bright Side

A Mother's Story of Love and Healing
through Her Daughter's Autism

suzie carpenter

Foreword by Patricia C. Kane, PhD

Writers of the Round Table Press
PO Box 511, Highland Park, IL 60035
www.roundtablecompanies.com

Publisher: *Corey Michael Blake*
President: *Kristin Westberg*
Executive Editor: *Francesca Crozier-Fitzgerald*
Creative Director: *Sunny DiMartino*
Project Manager: *Leeann Sanders*
Facts Keeper: *Mike Winicour*
Cover Design: *Sunny DiMartino*
Interior Design: *Christy Bui*
Proofreading: *Adam Lawrence*
Last Looks: *Carly Cohen*

Printed in the United States of America

First Edition: November 2016
10 9 8 7 6 5 4 3 2 1

Library of Congress Cataloging-in-Publication Data
Carpenter, Suzie.
On the bright side: a mother's story of love and healing through her daughter's autism / Suzie Carpenter.—1st ed. p. cm.
ISBN Paperback: 978-1-939418-89-0
ISBN Digital: 978-1-939418-90-6
Library of Congress Control Number: 2016956690

RTC Publishing is an imprint of Writers of the Round Table, Inc. Writers of the Round Table Press and the RTC Publishing logo are trademarks of Writers of the Round Table, Inc.

For Kelly: you are the bright side.

And for mothers everywhere: remember you are never alone.

Each chapter in this book opens with a short reflection.

These are Kelly's prophetic insights.

Contents

foreword

Our lives are journeys that ebb and flow with twists and turns, laughter and tears. This is a story of an extraordinary mother and her supreme effort to find the answers to bring her daughter out of the grip of autism and into the light.

For most parents, the diagnosis of autism is an overwhelming challenge as there are so many diverse opinions on how to manage the disorder. Many people believe that it is easy to address autism with applied behavior analysis (ABA) therapy, using a gluten-free/casein-free diet, fish oil, or "chelation." Others promote medication. These Band-Aid modalities and many more have failed in bringing children out of autism.

Ten years ago, a precious little girl, Kelly, and her mother, Suzie Carpenter, visited me. I knew from the moment I met Kelly that she was suffering terribly, yet she was a strong, beautiful, bright child who just needed a guide to peel off the coat of autism. I also knew by interacting with her mother that she was incredibly loving and supportive of Kelly, which is half the battle since a parent who is able to follow through with nutritional suggestions is crucial to the healing process.

Kelly had severely impaired gastrointestinal function that had not been addressed appropriately since, at that time, there was a poor understanding of the microbiome/neurological connection in children with autism.

Autism is a neurological illness rooted in disturbed phospholipid metabolism, often occurring after a toxic insult resulting in altered epigenetics. Each child with autism has a unique set of symptoms, strengths, and weaknesses. One cannot line up two children diagnosed with autism and categorize them similarly. To reach each child we must approach them as individuals and apply therapy that uniquely addresses their needs, starting at a cell membrane level.

Kelly is a symbol for each of us that we can reach for a star, that there is always hope that we can reach far enough to find our way out of the darkness, which, in Kelly's case, was autism.

In the process of blossoming, Kelly was quite outspoken regarding what helped her, and without question phospholipids were paramount in her recovery process. Kelly's mother Suzie stood firmly by her throughout her journey, surrounding her daughter with love and light, believing in her, and willing to try anything within reason to help her child. Suzie, not surprisingly, learned a great deal about herself and spread her own wings as she worked diligently to find answers for her child.

As the emergence of robust medical literature and clinical findings have expanded our understanding of autism, we have learned to superbly address the lipid disturbances, microbiome imbalance, neuroinflammation, and epigenetics of autism. Yet there is also something supremely important in the healing process: it's called unconditional love. As this mother and daughter struggled to find a way out of autism, love guided their way.

Patricia C. Kane, PhD
NeuroLipid Research Foundation
Millville, New Jersey
Summer 2016

The stories in this book reflect the author's experiences, as she remembers them, in her perspective. Some names and locations have been changed to respect the privacy of those individuals depicted in the book. The dialogue in this book has been re-created from memory and journal entries.

This book is not intended to be read as a substitute for medical advice or recommendations of practicing physicians. All readers are encouraged to consult his or her physician regularly in matters relating to his or her health, especially in regards to symptoms that may require diagnosis or medical attention.

1

a mother's dream

"Find what you love and hold on to it."

As soon as the nurse handed me my baby, the swaddled seven-pound bundle that had been living inside me for almost nine months, I surrendered to love.

Just moments before, the clattering of stainless steel and concert of voices in the sterile, white linoleum floored hospital room had all carefully orchestrated her safe delivery. My obstetrician handed Scott a pair of scissors and asked if he wanted to cut the baby's umbilical cord. Scott's forehead wrinkled in surprise. *Really me?* He hesitated briefly, then made the cut, deliberately, with pride. His heart-shaped lips cast a playful, proud grin. He was now the father of two blonde, blue-eyed daughters, both twenty-one inches long at birth.

The voices echoing around me faded as I unraveled the swaddling blanket to see and feel the miracle of our second child, Kelly Marie Carpenter. The unblemished, chamois-soft skin of her tiny toes rubbing against the palm of my hand made my skin prickle with joy. My eyes adoringly scanned over her long, skinny arms and legs that had kicked and nudged me for the past thirty-eight weeks—a thrilling sensation of life within. She smelled of warm towels, fresh out of the dryer. Clean, new life.

A few hours after Kelly was born, my mom brought Natalie to

the hospital to meet her new baby sister. I glanced over at Natalie, two years old, and gazed into her perfectly round, big, blue eyes. Then I shifted to Kelly, just born, and I made a silent pact with myself. I would do everything in my power to protect my girls—brace their falls, dodge schoolyard bullies, feed their healthy and growing young bodies. Things would go wrong; that was inevitable. When it did, I'd hug them so hard that the hurt would pass from their body into mine. They were my babies, my treasured pearls, and now they each had a sister. They'd always have me, they'd always have Scott, and they'd always have each other.

In my very first memory, I am eighteen months old. The recollection is so vivid that I can feel the sadness all over again. Sitting on a chair outside my parents' bedroom I waited with my tiny hands resting quietly in my lap. I was silent, not a peep. When I looked up and saw my mother walking toward me, her eyes were fixated on the baby cradled in the crook of her arm.

Before she delivered my baby sister, I'd watched my mom's belly grow larger. With a baby occupying the space that used to be mine, I sensed a change coming. When she went into labor, the idea of my mom being away at the hospital worried my one-year-old brain. *When will she be back? Will she be okay? Will she still be able to take care of me?*

In the hallway walking toward me, alongside my mom, was a baby nurse. As they approached, my mother didn't seem to notice me. I wished she would glance over, smile, then reach out and gently touch me with her hand. My eyes squinted and stung as I fought back tears. Everything around me suddenly became irrelevant. I stared at my hands, then hugged my arms close to my belly. Suddenly, I was a nobody. Everyone's attention was on the new baby. I imagine it was just like it had been for my two older sisters when I was born. The images are fuzzy, the thoughts fleeting, but the feeling is there. I felt abandoned, placed to the side for the time being—a feeling that stayed with me for many years.

I am the middle of five sisters with six and a half years between the oldest and youngest. As a child, I couldn't appreciate the challenges my mom had to face. She had a husband who believed house chores and child-rearing were the woman's business, who wanted a pleasant, energetic wife to mend the house, while still reserving time and space for him at the end of the day.

To her credit, she also managed to get out of the house to play golf several times a week and to volunteer on boards for local nonprofits like the Art Institute and Reading Hospital. The way things looked from where I sat, my mom had time to play golf and please my father, her friends, and volunteer comrades, but was left with very little time for me and my sisters. At least that was how I felt as a young girl.

Even when my mom was home with us, she was usually preoccupied with other things. She'd tinker around the house, chat on the phone with friends or committee members, then freshen up and prepare a family dinner before dad got home. I could see she had enough going on. She didn't need extra pestering. Sometimes I'd just watch silently from the kitchen table, amazed at how many things she was calculating in her mind at once. I'd imitate the habit by finding long lists of chores and responsibilities to tend to around the house.

"Suzie's staying home to play with her dollies," my father would tease me in a high-pitched, whiny tone that sounded like boys badgering each other on the playground. That was how he'd try to motivate me to stop playing house and go outside with my sisters to ride bikes or run around. But I liked playing house. My innate maternal instinct was shining through. The predictable, purposeful nature of domestic chores soothed me and gave me a sense of effortless accomplishment.

When I was five or six years old, I eagerly volunteered to help the babysitter iron my dad's handkerchiefs. I'd stand on a stool so

I could reach the ironing board and delighted in the transformation of a wrinkled ball of cotton ironed into a perfect, flat white square. Spraying the starch and then hearing the hot iron sizzle as it smoothed the fabric, making all the wrinkles disappear, was like magic.

Vacuuming was a similar phenomenon. Once I was a little older, our live-in babysitter, Jane, who also cleaned the house, showed me how to vacuum. Ours was an Electrolux canister vacuum with an attachment for rugs and one for hardwood or tile floors. Jane taught me how to remove the attachment and use the vacuum wand to suck up any dirt, dust bunnies, or bugs from the crevices between the wall and the edge of the carpeting. Our kitchen floor had red wall-to-wall carpeting which showed every crumb. I vacuumed it often.

When I was ten, my favorite game was playing "restaurant." I pretended I was a waitress with a full dining room. With an apron around my waist, I'd take my family's orders with a little pad of paper and pencil. Then I hurried off to our kitchen to play chef, cooking meals from the menu I'd created—hamburgers, buttered noodles, or scrambled eggs.

At that time, we lived in a large stucco house, painted pale yellow with a green-tile Spanish roof. My sisters and I each had our own bedroom. Mine was right next to my mom's bathroom. When I heard the bath water running, I'd quietly tiptoe in to see her, knowing I'd have her complete attention. And when she wasn't there, I'd sneak in just to marvel at her collection of antique glass perfume bottles on the ledge by her sink.

Our house was home to seven people, yet I often felt alone. Over time and by experience, I determined that if I needed someone to talk to or wanted to learn about girl stuff like tampons, tweezing my eyebrows, or kissing a boy, my sisters were the ones who I'd turn to for advice. Or, worst case scenario, I'd figure it out on my own. I remember thinking that when I have children, I will make them feel special, seen and heard.

Of course, this was probably every girl's vision of motherhood—being a renaissance mom, keeping your own life together, running the household, giving undivided attention to each child, not accounting for all the things that can be out of your control.

In my young mind, I had it all perfectly laid out. My handsome prince, tall with dark hair and blue eyes, would waltz into the room, swoop me up, and we'd live happily ever after. We'd be partners in life, sharing our dreams, parenting together, and our kids would think I was the best mom on the block. This was the romantic vision of my future that floated around my teenage mind. I hung on to that idealistic dream even as a young woman.

My fairy tale fantasy came true in 1991 when I was twenty-four years old and married Scott. Scott and I met in 1983, vacationing on Nantucket, where both of our families spent summers. The first time we saw each other, I was wearing a Lilly Pulitzer bikini. I remember it perfectly—the navy blue fabric sprinkled with magenta pink flowers, bandeau top, and ties at my hips. My skin glistened a rich golden tan, and my hair, an unruly set of shiny, light-brown curls, danced on the top of my head. Scott was taller than I'd imagined my prince to be, but I liked the way he carried his six-foot-six frame with strength and confidence. At sixteen, I was entering my senior year in high school, and at eighteen, Scott was going to be a sophomore in college.

Being with Scott was easy and comfortable. It was like we'd known each other all along, in another life perhaps. He made me laugh like no one else ever could. It was spontaneous, carefree. We'd talk for hours on end, his deep blue eyes focused on mine as if nothing else existed in the whole world but the two of us. This refreshing, relaxed romance was something I'd never experienced before. Right from the beginning, I believed it was true love.

But we were young, and it was complicated. Ours was a summer romance, weaving in and out of eight years, the last four of which we didn't see each other at all. Then, Labor Day weekend of 1990, we were finally reunited on Nantucket. Magically, we effortlessly picked up right where we'd left off. Eight months later, on May 18, 1991, we were married.

"From now on, no matter what challenges you face in your life together, Scott, you are number one in Suzie's life, and Suzie, you are number one in Scott's life."

The words of the minister at our wedding replayed in my mind. From the moment I said, "I do," with resounding confidence, my body was in a waltz of calm, purposeful joy. Getting married to Scott felt like coming home. It was natural, easy, comfortable.

As newlyweds, we were crazy for each other and busy building our careers. Even though I had to be at work by seven a.m. and didn't get back home until six p.m., I enjoyed making dinner for the two of us every night. It delighted me to cook and serve meals with gifts we'd gotten from our wedding—all the new kitchen tools, pots, pans, serving dishes, china, and silverware. I was finally playing house in my very own home—well, apartment actually, but it was still a stage for me to perform all the grown-up household activities that I'd imitated as a child.

Just as we'd settled into married life together, my dad wrote Scott a letter convincing him to come work for the family business, Bachman Snacks, a manufacturer of pretzels, chips, and Jax Cheese Curls. Together, Scott and I decided it was a once-in-a-lifetime opportunity.

So in November of 1991, I left my career at Dun & Bradstreet and Scott left his career at Cushman & Wakefield to move from northern New Jersey to Wyomissing, Pennsylvania. While the move was clearly about grooming Scott to run the business someday, I was also offered a job working in the credit department. Slightly rocked by culture shock, having moved from the glitzy corporate culture of the metropolitan New York area to rural Pennsylvania, we tried keeping our minds on the bigger picture of our future.

For our first wedding anniversary, six months after moving, Scott gave me a Waterford crystal statue of the number one to symbolize the commitment we'd keep to one another. It was about six inches tall and delicately etched in classic Waterford crystal style. When Scott bought it, his friend who was with him thought it was a ridiculous gift. He teased Scott and told him that I would be disappointed, assuming I'd prefer jewelry over something with pure sentimental value. He was wrong. I loved my number one.

In September of 1992, we moved into our first home, fully renovated with my dream kitchen, all new bathrooms, refinished hardwood floors, a new roof, and a fresh coat of paint everywhere. It was a few miles from my parents and only a block away from my childhood home—the yellow stucco house with the green roof. We'd made new friends, entertained a lot, and worked long hours for the family business.

One cold, lazy Saturday morning in November, almost two years into our marriage, we lingered in bed under the cozy, warm covers. Scott rolled over to his side, facing me, and asked if I wanted to start a family, to have kids. It wasn't the first time we talked about it, but this time was different.

As we lay there, we imagined our lives together on either side of that choice. In a life without children, we could travel anywhere. Our time would be our own. We could be selfish, focus completely on our love for one another, and wouldn't have to juggle all the responsibilities of parenting. The idea of a romantic partnership without kids trailing behind us, wiping their noses, sounded glamorous to me. It felt like a relief, easy. Sure, the idea of kids was nice for someday in the future, but I didn't think I was ready for that responsibility. Not yet.

Then, unexpectedly, Scott sat up and blurted out, "I think we should start trying to get pregnant," as if he'd already had a full conversation inside his head that I couldn't hear; like he'd already done his own analysis that led to a different conclusion.

He continued, "If something ever happens to me, I want to leave a part of me with you."

My body went limp, every muscle, every sensation centered in utter, complete love. Inside, I tingled all over with a warm, fuzzy feeling that allowed me to forget all about planning, timing, or logistics. That one sentence, full of romance, completely changed my idea of having children. I'd never thought of it that way. Now, instead of a presumed next step or burden to my body, the idea of having kids was about the creation of life that we'd complete together with pieces of both of us united in a new being. For the first time since we got married, I knew that if we could be ready together, I could be ready.

It took five months to conceive, though it seemed more like a year. I became obsessed with fertilizing my egg, foolishly thinking I could manipulate the timing and its exact coordinates. I thought I could control the whole process. Learning otherwise was a humbling and valuable lesson in the miracle of life. When the soft tickling sensation fluttered down low in my stomach, the first real sign of life inside me, I looked up to the sky. *Thank you.* Motherhood was the best gift I would receive.

Naturally, pregnancy exhausted me. It felt like pulling an all-nighter when all you want to do is eat, thinking it will make you more alert and present. I was still working full time and naps were only a weekend luxury. Eating energized me and helped calm the nausea that went beyond morning sickness and lasted all day.

My appetite was insatiable. I began eating off Scott's plate instead of him eating off mine. It felt like I had a hole in my stomach and no matter how much I ate, I never got full. I craved carbs and fried foods. For lunch, I gobbled entire meatball subs with french fries, and dinner usually consisted of big bowls of buttered pasta or full plates of meat and potatoes. Without a thought to how much weight I might gain or the health of our baby, I ate whatever I felt like eating. I had no appetite for healthy foods like salads or vegetables, and no discipline to force myself to eat them just because the so-called pregnancy bible, *What to Expect When You're Expecting*, said I should.

It was the opposite with alcohol. I didn't have one single drop during pregnancy. My taste buds and stomach developed an aversion to alcohol of any kind. Even the word *wine* made me nauseous.

Four weeks before my due date, a routine ultrasound showed the baby was breech. A cesarean section was scheduled for three weeks later on Wednesday, January 26, 1994. The night before, on the eve of our future as parents, we went out to dinner to celebrate the end of married life without children and to decide on our baby's name.

We chose a name with grace, sophistication, and beauty for our first baby girl. Natalie Farrell Carpenter was born healthy and warm on that snowy wintery morning.

When it was time to go home from the hospital, I wasn't ready. My face was white as a ghost, my stomach was queasy, and I could barely stand. The spinal headache I'd been warned about hit me hard, and the throbbing pain in my head was crippling. This was one of the unpleasant and relatively rare side effects of the spinal tap procedure, the anesthesia of choice with a cesarean section. I got dressed anyway and collapsed into the hospital wheelchair.

Moments later, I was back at home with my first baby girl, Natalie. Too sick to even celebrate motherhood, my hand gripped the railing as I slowly climbed up the stairs to my room, then promptly crawled into my bed, crumbling into a fetal position under the covers. Nothing existed except for me, my baby, and my pain.

That was until I heard a loud pop coming from the kitchen. It was a familiar sound, but not a welcomed one—the cork of a bottle of champagne followed by laughter and loud talking. My parents, Scott's parents, and Scott were all downstairs in the kitchen, celebrating the birth of Natalie, our beautiful baby girl now sleeping next to our bed in a hand-painted white wicker bassinet. The thought of joining them was far from my mind. In fact, I wished they would all just shut up. I closed my eyes and put a pillow over my head, hoping the pain and noise would go away.

The gripping headache lasted over two weeks. While I was bedridden, my mom held my newborn baby as if she were her own. She rocked Natalie gently by my bedside in a light-brown antique wood rocking chair she'd brought over from her house. It was my grandfather's old rocking chair, one that I bet she'd been rocked in as a baby years ago.

As I lay helpless in bed, a new mother unable to care for her own baby, my mom came to my rescue. She changed Natalie's diapers, helped me while I struggled to nurse Natalie, and brought me meals in bed. Her companionship and undivided attention took my mind off the pain. My mom had always been a good cook and made the best homemade soups. To pass the time, she and I would fantasize about starting a soup company one day, that we could open together and keep in the family for years. Every day, we'd design this dream together.

During those horrible transition weeks, my mom decided Natalie and I were her top priority—something she couldn't do when I was a little girl. I believe it nursed me back to health. After almost three weeks, the spinal headache disappeared. Finally, I could fully soak up the joys of motherhood.

As Natalie grew over the next year and a half, she became my best little buddy. At eighteen months old, her hand in mine, we'd skip down the street giggling, blissfully content in endearing moments. Her little body snuggled next to mine, she listened intently to me or Scott read her stories. At such a young age, Natalie had an intellectual curiosity that impressed and intrigued me. If I changed a word or skipped a line in the storybook, she'd correct me, laughing. It was a little game between the two of us.

Natalie focused on tasks with an interest beyond her age. I'd watch her sit on the kitchen floor, making pretend soup with a large metal bowl, wooden spoon, and some dried beans. Her concentration was incredible, as if she believed she was a real chef making real soup. It filled me with pride and joy to let her experiment, explore, and discover. Unlike other children her age, she didn't know who Barney or Elmo were because there was never a need to watch television. Well, at least that was true until I got pregnant again.

One sunny September day, I opened the back door to carry the garbage out to the garage. Natalie was drawing pictures with crayons and singing a silly song in the room next to the kitchen that faced the garage and backyard. I walked down the stairs on the path to the garage and placed the garbage in the can. When I started walking back toward the room where I'd left Natalie coloring, I doubled over, cringing from a putrid smell—the recognizable scent of a dead animal. I looked down and saw the miniature corpse of a mole, a present from our beloved black and white Maine coon cat, Pepé Le Pew.

The stench passed through my nostrils, into my throat, making me gag. Queasiness set in. It was a familiar kind of nausea, and I knew only one thing could create this type of response. I was pregnant again.

Pregnancy was not in our plan this time. The news threw me off guard. I wasn't sad or disappointed, but it felt like too much all at once; like a frustrating dream where I was ready to run but my legs wouldn't move; like I wanted to scream but I had no voice. The realization intensified in the weeks after I found out. Instead of feeling blessed with new life, I'd wake up in a sweat, heart racing, panting for air.

I believed that I could only handle one child. Whether or not it was true, I'd convinced myself that I only had enough love to fully love and adore Natalie alone. The minute the number grew to two or more children, I worried the first one wouldn't feel loved anymore. Anxiety and fear overshadowed the miracle inside me—reflections of the way I'd felt as a little girl.

Again, Scott helped me to shift my perspective. He was excited, explaining that now Natalie wouldn't have to be an only child. She'd have a playmate and a best friend. He felt she deserved at least one sibling, and somewhere inside, I knew he was right.

So there I was, nine months later on May 9, 1996, holding our second baby girl, Kelly Marie Carpenter. Once again, my mother came to my rescue, watching Natalie around the clock while Scott and I endured the labor contractions as a team. After over thirty-six hours of labor and multiple trips to the hospital, I was able to have a vaginal delivery.

Kelly's birth was the most thrilling experience I'd ever had in my life. The rush of adrenaline post-delivery was extraordinary. Relieved beyond belief, I walked out of the hospital the next day with a victorious bounce in my step. I felt so good. Though I was tired from the endless hours of labor, I felt like myself, emotionally and energetically. Like a rebirth, it signified my ability to do it all—to be a loyal wife, a loving daughter, and to fulfill my childhood dream of being a devoted, adoring mother. The role I believed was my destiny.

When Natalie was a baby, for the first three months, she cried inconsolably for several hours every single night. Thinking it was colic, we took her to the pediatrician who explained that she was fine.

"The good news is that you have a highly intelligent child. She's merely over-stimulated from all the things she sees and hears all day long. Then at night, she breaks down," Dr. Smith told us. "She can't handle any more stimulation, and it makes it hard for her to fall asleep." He described Natalie to a tee.

Now, two years later, baby Kelly was the opposite of her big sister Natalie. Kelly was quiet, rarely fussed, and slept a lot. I'd made the decision to not breastfeed the second time around, which I found to be so much easier. The bouncy chair was Kelly's favorite place. With a big grin on her face, she was perfectly content to rock for hours by herself. Scott and I joked that we should have named her Happy.

That was until she turned two.

2

something's not right

"We are all weird in our own ways, which is a great thing because we are all different."

I had no idea that anything was wrong with Kelly. I just thought that this was how she's supposed to be. It never occurred to me that her head was larger than other toddlers' heads, that her incessant rocking was unusual, or that she didn't babble like other babies.

"You know, I've been thinking, maybe you should get Kelly's hearing checked. She's two years old and she still isn't talking. Don't you think that's strange?" my mom prodded.

Starting as early as eighteen months old, Natalie blurted out long sentences, stringing together a precocious vocabulary. Like a game, at the dinner table, my sister would say a word and ask Natalie to repeat it. Then they'd giggle together at the ease with which Natalie could pronounce the words.

I'd been making a conscious effort to avoid comparing Natalie and Kelly, loving them individually as their own unique selves. Yet, reflecting on where Natalie was at the same age as Kelly showed the drastic difference in the pace and complexity of their development.

I didn't think Kelly was deaf as my mom hypothesized, so I resisted the maternal nudge to get her hearing checked. Though it was delayed, language gradually developed for Kelly. By the time she reached three years old, her words awkwardly formed into short sentences or demands. Then, slowly but surely, our quiet

13

and happy baby started to show signs of distress when speaking often turned into screaming.

Disturbingly obstinate and dramatically unusual behaviors began creeping into our lives by the time Kelly was three and a half years old. With every transition, like bedtime, meal time, or going to preschool, Kelly's expressive skinny arms thrashed, often throwing things while she bawled in protest. Her wrists were thin and her fingers long, making her movements more dramatic in a graceful but distressing way.

As a toddler, Kelly's hair was wispy and a beautiful light blonde color. It was the hair I'd always wished I had. Her eyes were smaller than Natalie's but the same deep, dark blue color like the ocean. Her nose was small and round as a button, and her petal-pink lips were extremely expressive when she either smiled a distant smile or growled in frustration. Kelly was a beautiful little girl with a spirit that had a mind of its own.

"You stupid, Mommy. I don't like you!" Kelly hollered while darting me an evil look and eloping from my request that she come eat breakfast. Despite her precious exterior, something inside Kelly was making her angry and agitated.

Right before lunch, she begged, "Can I have an ice cream sandwich?"

"No," I firmly answered. "Ice cream sandwiches are for dessert."

In protest, Kelly threw her body onto the floor and banged her fists on the carpet as she yelled over and over again, "I don't like you, you're a crooked mommy."

It made no sense, but the message was clear. I knew she was upset. These outbursts would happen every day, as often as fifteen times a day, with every transition or demand.

Sometimes, when I picked her up from Montessori, Kelly refused to leave. A couple of times, with a firm grip on her hand, I tried leading her out of school, but she pulled her hand free from mine and plopped down on the carpet in front of the two glass doors at the entrance of the school. Without any luck, I'd end up peeling her off the floor. When another mom walked by, hand-in-hand with her docile child, I pretended to smile as if Kelly's behavior was so outrageous that it might actually be funny.

After finally arriving at the car, I opened the door, wiped the crumbs off her car seat, and moved the buckles out of the way so she could easily jump into it. This time, her objection was adamant and particularly concerning.

"It has a line in it! It has a line in it!" she yelled at the top of her range. "No!" she screeched as I lifted her up and placed her into the seat, buckling her without asking. The crying did not stop from that point until we got home. Natalie and I tried to ignore it, but Kelly was rocking her entire body back and forth, charging her head backward into the seat, shaking the whole vehicle.

"I don't want to hear any sounds," Kelly commanded.

In that moment, a switch flipped for me. Something was not right. This was not the normal terrible twos or threes. This was not your typical toddler obstinacy. Something was bothering Kelly deep within her core, and she did not know how to tell us. Feeling helpless, my skin prickled with fear. I tried to take slow, deep breaths. *Just get home for now. Just get to the house.* Then Kelly snapped again, trying to reach her sister with her hand.

"I can't see Natalie's face!"

Natalie sat silently looking out the car window.

Connecting to our kitchen was a little sitting room with a bookcase that housed baskets of crayons, coloring books, paper, and other arts and crafts. A small television sat on a table in the corner. At the opposite side of the room was a door that led out to our modest square backyard, framed by arborvitaes. In the middle of the room was a wooden kitchen table that used to be Scott's grandmother's. It was just large enough for four chairs, and its shiny protective finish made it easy to clean—a perfect surface to let the girls experiment with paint, clay, markers, or glue. Scott often sat at the same table to eat dinner with his grandparents when he was a child. Now, Natalie and Kelly ate there. While *Arthur* or some other PBS show played in the background, the girls sat to do their crafts.

One day, while I was washing dishes at the kitchen sink and Kelly was sitting at the table coloring, I heard the back door open followed by the glass storm door banging shut. I assumed Kelly had gotten up and was going to the backyard to play. Seconds later, I looked out the kitchen window and saw her sitting in the middle of the street, legs crossed, staring off into space. I turned off the sink and ran out the back door. By the time I got to Kelly, my neighbor was there, talking to Kelly calmly in her grandmotherly way. Withholding any explanation, I thanked her and led Kelly inside with a tight grip on her hand while she tugged at my arm, resisting and resenting the interruption.

While most children don't fully grasp limits or understand boundaries and consequences, they typically fear them when they're getting too close. Usually they can think ahead and imagine a bad outcome or recognize the sensation of fear in their body—like a sudden, sharp inhale, a racing heartbeat, or the subtle urge to urinate or throw up. Plus, they learn from experience—being yelled at or getting hurt. Kelly had no sense of danger. It was as if she didn't grasp that certain sequences of events lead to the possibility of peril.

This made Kelly appear fearless. She didn't seem to have the same ability to hesitate and assess a situation, to consider it dangerous or not. She wouldn't stop before jumping into the pool and wonder if she could swim or not. She wouldn't stop herself from running full speed toward the top of the staircase without considering the height. To Kelly, the street was a place to sit and look up at the trees. She missed the bigger picture—the danger—and the surrounding details.

I wondered why did she fear sleeping, facial expressions, and interacting with others, and yet not see the danger in getting hit by a car, drowning, or falling off a boulder at the edge of a cliff?

Kelly lived inside her own body, in her world, without realizing what was going on around her. If we tried to explain how she could injure herself or others, her head nodded, but it wasn't sinking in. It scared me and Scott. Many nights, I'd wake up to my heart racing after the recurring nightmare of Kelly drowning in a pool or breaking away from my hand, darting into the parking lot and getting hit by a car.

During the fall of Kelly's second year of preschool, when she was three and a half years old, I got an unexpected phone call from the school's office manager.

"Cindy would like to meet with you, Kathy, and Maria," she said in a friendly, business-like tone. Cindy was the director of the school. Kathy and Maria were Kelly's teachers.

"Sure," I responded, exhaling a grateful breath that the call wasn't about an accident, sickness, or some emergency. I resisted the temptation to ask why. Even though I wanted to know more, I resigned myself to the fact that I'd find out soon enough.

I had recently gone back to work full time for my family's business, Bachman Snacks, where Scott still also worked. Since Natalie was born, I'd been overseeing the company's retail store from home. Now, since the numbers weren't stacking up, I needed to jump in and figure out why. The cost of goods sold was inexplicably high and profits were down significantly. To cut costs, I decided to fire the manager and do the job myself. Once I stepped in, I learned that he had a drinking problem and had been stealing money from the store. Even though I doubted them at first, my instincts were spot on. Something was not quite right.

Having Natalie and Kelly in school together was key. The babysitter could get them from the same place and stay with them in the afternoon and early evening hours while Scott and I were both still at work.

I was exhausted by the time I got home at night, physically and emotionally. Most of the day, I was on my feet either at the register, stocking shelves, or rotating product code dates. I was constantly worried about waste, sales, and inventory numbers. Not trusting anyone else to handle the cash, I opened the store in the morning and closed the store at night. In my gut, I knew this attention to detail mattered, even if it was wearing me out to the point of being unable to give anything to anyone else.

If there was going to be a problem with Kelly at school, the timing could not have been worse. On the day of the meeting, I arrived by myself with a notebook in hand.

"Good morning," I said casually to the office manager who was sitting at her desk focusing on the stack of papers in front of her.

"Good morning," she echoed. With a polite grin, she looked up at me, offering hospitality laced with subtle empathy. I imagined she was thinking, *Oh, it's you.* After some small talk about how beautiful it was outside, she walked me down the hall to a large conference room that I'd never been in.

Kelly's teachers, Kathy and Maria, sat at the middle of a long, wooden table. Cindy, the school director who was also Natalie's teacher, and a few other teachers that worked with Kelly during the day were also sitting around the table. I entered the room and all eyes were on me. Eyes that oozed pity, empathy, and bad news.

I scrambled to process what was happening. Every inch of my body retracted, anticipating a blow. I sat down with the weight of five people. *Did I do something wrong? What have I missed?* Their faces were kind, and concerned. It's not that I felt judged so much as left out. I avoided eye contact, looking up around the walls, back down at my lap. *Where are the windows?* The walls appeared dirtier and greyer with each passing minute. In moments, I'd be run over by a wayward truck I'd never seen coming.

"Suzie, we all love Kelly," Cindy said, capturing my gaze. "We all want to see her get the help she needs."

Help? What kind of help? The look on my face mirrored my

confusion and terror. I felt a knot, a thousand questions, rising up in my throat. I said nothing. My body began to tense up as if it had something to tell me or as if it wanted to protect me.

Kelly's teachers began to share stories about what was happening in the classroom. Kelly wouldn't listen to any instructions or demands and was often unresponsive to attempts to engage her in a lesson or conversation. Clapping to get her attention made no impact on her blank, unresponsive stare. Kathy and Maria said it was as if Kelly didn't hear the clapping, even when it was right in front of her face. Kelly's blue eyes were empty, distant. It was like she came from a different planet than the other children. They recounted the handful of times that she wandered out of the classroom and into the hallway, in a trance.

Maria was an excellent complement to Kathy who was the more rigid of the two teachers. We got to know and love Maria when she was Natalie's preschool teacher and requested that Kelly be in her class. Like the pied piper, Maria led children in song and dance. Always smiling and hugging them, she got to know each child individually as if their hopes and dreams had become her own.

Maria exuded the warmth of a loving grandmother with an easy style that welcomed all. Rising only four feet, ten inches off the floor without heels, her stature made it easier to nestle as many children as possible. Kelly cooed over her colorful dresses, chunky heeled shoes, and shiny, bobbly jewelry. Maria was the only one who could engage Kelly. She sang to Kelly in her soft, Mexican accent and somehow hypnotized Kelly to follow her lead and instruction.

I took my left hand and placed it over my right to stop the tap-tap-tapping. I hoped they wouldn't notice. *Why won't they just tell me what they're thinking? Why all this build up?* Each story points to only one thing: Kelly's not "normal." But they don't want to give it a name. They don't want to guess or scare me, but I can see them biting their tongues. That scares me more.

They continued. The contrast is stark. Next to twenty other children, Kelly doesn't act like any of them, they said.

"Don't you see it at home?" Cindy asked.

"Not exactly," I responded blankly.

Up until now, I'd thought Kelly's issues were resolvable, that over time they'd go away if we just used a different approach. It never crossed my mind that she was in a different class of kids—the ones that ride the special little yellow school bus and have their own classroom.

Cindy assured me they were not kicking her out of school.

"Of course Kelly can stay," she reassured. Kathy and Maria chimed in. They had their hands full, but they cared about Kelly and wanted to help. They reiterated that Kelly was not engaged, was not learning, was struggling socially, and needed to get help.

Whiplash typically occurs in one swift smack, creating a paralyzing state of shock. The only difference here was that I was getting it in small, consecutive blows, one after the other, knocked down every time another teacher opened her mouth. I was standing in the way of an endlessly rotating windmill.

I wanted to respond, something to break the stiff air, but nothing came out. The same teachers that raved about Natalie's creativity, innate leadership, and precocious reading and writing skills were now telling me that something was wrong with Kelly—something beyond what I'd ever be able to handle on my own. The shock must have been written all over my face. As I fought tears back, Maria grabbed my hand as if letting me know she was there to walk this path with me.

"I think your first step would be to make an appointment with your pediatrician," Maria said. "See what they recommend."

I appreciated Maria's tip, but I didn't dare to speak for fear of launching into hysterics. She knew that. Tears made my eyes blurry. I nodded and forced a closed-lip smile.

Scott and I chose Montessori because they believe every child is unique and focus on each student's strengths, not deficits. There are no comparisons or measurements. With this model, learning is driven by the child. By building confidence and self-advocacy this way, the child doesn't have to fit in to a predetermined curriculum. The work is self-paced with very little or no classroom instruction, which makes it easier to deal with a child who doesn't learn incidentally or has trouble processing language. It would take me a long time to accept that Kelly was outside of this model, as free and limitless as it seemed.

I don't remember the car ride home. I needed time to process. *What the hell am I going to do? How am I ever going tell Scott?* My head was spinning as my thoughts swirled in so many different directions. Would this be the day I remembered as the worst day of my life? Or, would it be the best? Was this the beginning of the journey of finding Kelly? I wasn't ready to be positive so I stayed teetering between extreme debilitating worry and that other thing, the more pleasant option. That night, when I told Scott about the meeting, he questioned the teachers' speculation that something was wrong with Kelly.

"Are you sure they aren't overreacting?" he asked.

But who was I to judge at this point? I needed more information. The phrase, "She needs help," was on repeat in my mind. As the conversation ensued, Scott's handsome baritone voice relaxed and consoled me. We agreed not to panic. It was just a matter of time before we'd hear what the doctor had to say. We could wait. We'd have to get used to waiting.

3

the villain in the mirror

"We should not wonder what could have been. Instead, we should wonder what will be. Because what we want to do and what will happen is what really matters."

It took several weeks to get an appointment with our pediatrician to discuss Kelly's behavioral issues. In the time we were waiting, repetitive incidents and reflections woke me up to the reality that, yes, indeed something was wrong with Kelly, and it was wearing me down. The building anticipation made it increasingly difficult to be without answers.

A few days after the Montessori meeting, Kelly and I walked to the playground together. It was a beautiful, sunny fall afternoon, and Kelly was in a cheerful mood. Piles of brown, lifeless leaves crunched beneath our feet. When we reached the path leading to the playground, Kelly looked down the hill in the direction of the swings, slides, and teeter-totters, spotting a potential friend—a cute young girl about Kelly's age standing near the bottom of the hill with her mother. The two girls met each other's eyes, smiled, and skipped toward one another.

Once they were face to face, Kelly beamed with joy at the prospect of a playmate. Overexcited, she took her tiny right hand and slapped it hard onto the girl's chest. She meant to say, *Hi, let's play!* Naturally, it was not understood that way by the little girl or her mother.

The mother's dark, slanted eyes quickly went from Kelly to me, glaring at us like we were aliens before grabbing her daughter's hand and quickly walking off. The mom didn't say anything, but I could guess what she was thinking. *You are a bad mother. What's wrong with you and your daughter?*

Maybe this really was worse than I'd imagined. I started noticing more and more idiosyncrasies in Kelly's actions—sort of like when you're shopping for a car and you start noticing the details of all the cars around you or seeing more of the make or model you like, as if, all of the sudden, it's the only car on the road.

The following Saturday, Kelly's friend, Tessa, came over for a playdate. I watched as, without warning, Kelly lunged forward and snatched a toy right out of Tessa's hand.

"Kelly!" Embarrassed, I rolled my eyes in Tessa's direction and reprimanded Kelly. "Ask Tessa for the toy. Grabbing's not nice. Say you're sorry!"

Kelly wouldn't look at me or Tessa. I shivered on the inside, cringing with anticipation of the next blow. Kelly's shoulders slumped as she clenched her fists, warning me that she might hit me or Tessa. Instead, she grunted and grabbed another toy away from Tessa, then stormed out of the room. Tessa's mouth was open but no words came out. Standing next to where Tessa was sitting, I yelled for Kelly to come back. But she didn't. I attempted to hide my frustration with a fake smile.

"Sorry, Tessa," I apologized for Kelly, and tried to downplay the situation by asking Tessa a few questions like what her favorite toys were at her house.

Motivated to play with her friend, Kelly returned a few minutes later and handed the toy back to Tessa without a word. Tessa obliged Kelly by continuing to play by Kelly's rules for the remainder of the play date.

Whenever I'd put my glasses on, Kelly would yell at me.

"Mom, take your glasses off."

I only wore glasses at night when my eyes were tired or dry

from wearing contacts, and Kelly hated the way I looked in glasses. It was the same thing when I was cooking. Kelly didn't like my expression when I was concentrating.

She'd look at me confused: "Mom, why are you mad?" To her, my squished eyebrows and accentuated worry creases spelled anger.

"I'm not mad, Kelly. Just thinking," I'd calmly reply.

Even after I explained, she would repeatedly ask, raising her voice more with each time, "Mom, why are you mad?"

My neck and shoulder muscles clenched tight to suck in the frustration of her repetitive false accusations. I remained stoic to avoid escalating her antagonism. All it took was for a person to look slightly different—like me with my glasses or a friend's husband with very deep-set eyes—to send Kelly into a fit of fear.

"I don't like the way that lady looks. I hate her!"

Kelly would say things like this in the supermarket, at school about other parents, or at the park. Sometimes the fearful outburst was about something we couldn't even see or notice. Like the time she hollered, "Dad, there's a face in my mirror looking at me!" as if a villain was about to jump out of the reflection. Scott couldn't see anything other than her. Was she scared of her own reflection, a shadow, or some other image she saw that we weren't able to see?

It was reminiscent of a few months earlier when we were visiting Scott's parents in Florida and a similar wave of angst came over Kelly. Scott was golfing with his dad, and his mom took the girls and I to the pool. Kelly launched into one of her fearful fits, and I didn't know what to do. Since Scott's mom wasn't aware of the problems we'd been having, I tried to remove ourselves from the scene. Kelly and I sat on the steps of the shallow end while Natalie was swimming nearby. Kelly clutched her arm tight around mine, leaning into my body as she stared at the water.

"There are scary lines down there in the pool," Kelly growled in a syncopated, low tone, echoing the same fear over and over.

Panicked, her eyes fixed on the water as if there were a monster lurking beneath the surface. She clung to me, afraid to move from the steps. Meanwhile, Scott's mom was oblivious to the tantrum because she was sitting fully clothed under an umbrella, laughing and talking with friends. Even though I was relieved to not have to explain Kelly's irrational perseveration, I wanted to cry tears of lonely, helpless frustration.

With each passing day, before school, in the car on the way to Montessori, on the way home, then at night after work, it became glaringly obvious that our conventional approach wasn't working. No matter how hard we tried, we couldn't handle this on our own. We needed to get some answers from her pediatrician.

The one thing that made me realize I wasn't crazy was knowing that the Montessori teachers, experienced and educated in childcare and behavior, couldn't figure out how to reach Kelly, to engage her, or direct her like they could all the other children. In the afternoons while Natalie was still at school, Kelly stayed home with just the babysitter and all they did was watch Kelly's favorite movies. That was one time of day when Kelly was completely content, which was a huge relief.

When the day finally came for our pediatrician appointment, I walked into the doctor's office all by myself. We'd decided it would be best to speak to the doctor without Kelly present. Natalie and Kelly were in school while Scott was busy at work managing the daily route truck deliveries of pretzels, chips, and Jax Cheese Curls to area grocery stores.

A nurse took me right back to the "well" side of the doctor's office, the segregated section of exam rooms for annual checkups and discussions like mine. With high hopes, I was ready and willing to share the stories of our challenges—how time-outs weren't working, how Kelly didn't seem to hear me, her tantrums, and what Montessori told me.

When Dr. Smith came in the room, he greeted me by shaking my hand. Then, he crossed his arms over his chest and faced the chair I was sitting in as he leaned his back-side against the empty examination table covered with crisp, clean, white paper. After a few minutes of listening to me talk, his stare turned from curious to disinterested, as though he had heard enough and was ready to give me an answer before I even finished telling him everything on my list.

"She's just stubborn," Dr. Smith interrupted me in a very matter-of-fact way. "Make it hurt. Keep her in time-out longer," was his advice.

He reasoned that she needed to feel the consequences of her behavior with a stronger, more painful separation from her environment. As he looked at me, he must have seen the expression of concern on my face as I nodded, hesitantly. Shell-shocked, I couldn't find the words I wanted to say. I wasn't convinced he was wrong, but questioned how would this possibly work when she so happily sat during time-out? I also wasn't convinced her behaviors were intentional and deserved punishment, even if they were inappropriate, disturbing, and exhausting.

I felt foolish. I'd waited all that time for an explanation, a diagnosis of some sort, and put all my eggs in one basket—Dr. Smith's basket. Surely, I assumed, he would know what was wrong, he'd have all the answers, he'd make recommendations, and I'd be on my way. I was wrong. It wasn't going to be that way at all.

With a quick, almost curt smile and his hands neatly shoved in the pockets of his khaki pants, he suggested we see a developmental pediatrician. *Okay. Sounds good, but what the heck is a developmental pediatrician?* I thought.

Dr. Smith's words swirled around in my head like a swarm of yellow jackets. His hasty dismissal and the way he minimized the situation made me doubt my maternal instincts. Could it be that simple, that Kelly was really just a stubborn kid? Was I a bad mom for failing to follow through long or hard enough? Maybe it was how I delivered the punishment, my tone of voice, or my facial expression. Was I too calm? Could it be true that Scott's parents were right about my parenting when Natalie was a toddler—that I was too nice and was spoiling her? Were they right when they said we told her we loved her too much, that we were gushing parents with no backbone? *Could this be all my fault?*

Excited to see me, knowing I'd just been to the doctor, Maria greeted me with enthusiasm as she stood inside the wooden split-rail fence that encompassed the Montessori school playground. Behind her, Kelly was running around in some sort of pattern or self-invented game while one of her classmates watched.

With Maria on one side of the fence and me on the other, I told her the story of my appointment with Dr. Smith. While I was proud of myself for seeking out an answer and asking for help, at the same time, I was confused by Dr. Smith's lack of empathy or professional respect for our struggle, and by his inability to offer innovative solutions. When I informed Maria that he'd said nothing was wrong with Kelly, Maria's lips parted, revealing the gap between two of her top front teeth. She gasped for air as her eyes widened in shock.

"No, that's not right. He obviously doesn't understand the full scope of what's going on here. If I were you I'd get another opinion." Maria's words were like those of a mother—gentle, but firm. Her hand gently touched my shoulder in compassion for our struggle.

"He referred us to a developmental pediatrician," I shared with her, as if it were a consolation prize. She agreed that was a good idea. There was still hope for an answer.

A few months later, when the day finally came for Kelly's appointment with the developmental pediatrician, I allowed plenty of time to prepare Kelly for our departure so we wouldn't be late. Another benefit of the extra time was that a successful, calm transition would keep me from showing her that I was anxious or worried. With just the two of us, it was also less complicated.

The developmental pediatrician only visited our pediatrician's office once a month. When Kelly and I walked into the designated exam room at the back of the doctor's office, he stood up to introduce himself. In a suit, tie, and white button-down shirt, he looked and acted in a businesslike fashion. After shaking my hand with very scant eye contact, he immediately sat back down at a table with a few large manuals, a note pad, and a pen. He instructed Kelly to sit in the chair facing him with her back to me.

Meanwhile, I perched myself in the cold, hard seat of a chair on the opposite wall. Without much explanation, the doctor began to check things off his list. He showed Kelly pictures or words and asked her questions about them—like what certain objects were, such as a dump truck, a lawn mower, a lion, and a tea cup, and whether or not they fit in a specified category. Kelly was surprisingly compliant almost as if she enjoyed the visual exercise.

Suddenly, it became clear that his tests were all about cognitive ability. Since we were more concerned about her escalating behaviors, my eyes began searching the room hoping maybe I'd missed something. Not wanting to interrupt his flow or disrupt Kelly, I kept quiet while he continued to work with her. Slumping into the plastic seat of the chair, my shoulders began to droop while I fidgeted with my fingers. Even though I decided to resign myself to waiting to hear what his results revealed, I had a sinking feeling that I'd still be left to my own devices. A few weeks later, when I called the pediatrician's office, they said that Kelly's test results were fairly insignificant, again leaving us without answers or strategies.

There was a tiny part of me that wondered if there really wasn't anything wrong with her after all. But that was just wishful thinking tightly swirled with denial. Rubbing my forehead over and over again with my fingers, I reminded myself that the way things were happening on the home front, there was no refuting that something was definitely wrong.

Every day, before and after school, there were multiple examples of perseveration, fear, confusion, and anger, whether it was just her and I alone together, her with Natalie, or her with Scott. It was like Kelly was falling deeper and deeper into a dark, scary hole.

Several weeks after the developmental pediatrician appointment, while I was still figuring out our next steps, Kelly got a bad cold. She had a cough, runny nose, and low fever. She wasn't sleeping, her nose was oozing green mucus, and her appetite waned.

"Mom, I have a yucky taste in my mouth," she protested, refusing to eat breakfast. Kelly wiped her nose with a tissue, frustrated that it was so congested and that the tissue wasn't making it better.

She screamed, "I hate my nose. Get this stuff out of my nose!" relentlessly rubbing her nose until it was bright red.

A few minutes later, when her hair fell into her face, she grabbed it with her fist and pulled hard on the clump of hair because she was so mad at feeling like she couldn't breathe.

Kelly then turned to me and said, "I don't like you, Mommy!" as if it was my fault she was sick.

I decided not to wait it out like I'd done with previous colds in the past and called the pediatrician's office. This appointment wasn't with Dr. Smith, but another doctor that we hadn't seen much before: Dr. Brown. He was on the shorter side, shorter than me, and had dark hair, a beard, and wore glasses. His soft brown eyes wrinkled around the edges and held my gaze, hinting at his compassion and concern.

Dr. Brown sat down, crossed his legs, and straightened his tie as if he he had nowhere else to go, patiently waiting to hear our story. While I had his attention, I decided to skip over Kelly's cold symptoms and asked his advice for how to deal with her behaviors. As I shared some examples with him, hoping for some kind of guidance, Kelly threw her body down on the two hard plastic chairs with shiny metal legs that leaned against the wall. She started crying loudly in protest, turning her face away from him and me.

Her expression screamed of confusion and betrayal. She yanked her pants down as she lay across the two chairs. Then she took her hands and began touching her bottom as if to comfort herself. I was totally embarrassed, but relieved at the same time. Maybe someone would finally understand there was something wrong.

Of all the odd, upsetting behaviors she engaged in, this was one I hadn't witnessed before. Dr. Brown silently watched her with curiosity and absence of judgment, as if he was examining what she was thinking, not just what she was doing. On some level, it was like he understood her pain, agony, and frustration. This allowed me to admit to him how, at times, I wanted to take my hands, place them on her shoulders, look her in the eye, and just shake her until the demon disappeared.

"Something's not right. I recommend you go see Dr. Robin Altman. She's a pediatric psychiatrist." He scribbled her name on the prescription pad, ripped off the white square piece of paper, and handed it to me. He also gave us a prescription for an antibiotic to treat Kelly's sinus infection.

For our first visit together, Dr. Altman requested to meet with all three of us—Scott, me, and Kelly. Scott and I walked into her office sharing the same eager anticipation. Even if it was a tiny thread at this point, hope was something we both clung to tightly; it bonded us together. As a couple, we were ready to participate, ask questions, get answers. Meanwhile, Kelly didn't know why we were there— what do you tell your kid when you are going to this kind of doctor?

Dr. Altman's office was large and inviting. Against one wall there was a large black leather couch with two matching chairs on either side that faced one another. To the right was a large play area with lots of toys for kids including a Playskool playhouse with a family of figurines and miniature plastic furniture. It was just like the Playmobil set that Kelly had at home, the one she played with every day. In the far corner of her office was Dr. Altman's desk and bookshelves stacked with books.

Scott and I sat on the black leather couch. He was at one end, and I was at the other. Guided by Dr. Altman, Kelly went over to the opposite side of the room and began playing with the toys. Then, Dr. Altman came and sat in a chair facing us. She crossed one leg over the other with her knee pointing away from us while her arms rested on the sides of the chair. Her figure was petite, barely five feet tall, and she had curly black hair cut in a neat, chic bob. Her relaxed smile stretched across her face.

"So, tell me about your concerns." Dr. Altman's unpretentious, laid-back approach told me she was not only curious to learn more of our story but also wanted to help. Scott turned his gaze my direction, allowing me to speak first. As I talked about the meeting I'd had with Kelly's teachers at Montessori, Dr. Altman listened intently, welcoming more details. She jotted down a few notes on her legal notepad. Every now and then, she glanced over at Kelly playing by herself and not paying any attention to our discussion about her.

There were moments when I felt like Dr. Altman was examining us as well. She wanted to know more about our family history, my family and Scott's. That was one topic that made me cringe. It didn't feel right to blame genetics for Kelly's situation. To me, it seemed like something more, and something that deserved attention beyond resignation to a predetermined destiny. Yet, not wanting to leave any stone unturned, I shared with Dr. Altman that my family did have a history of depression, and then also mentioned how Scott's mom had been having unpleasant panic attacks for a few years.

"Okay." She collected her thoughts and finished writing herself a note. "So, when would you say that things started to change or intensify with Kelly's behavior? Or was she always this way?" With all of her questions, Dr. Altman looked both of us in the eye, making sure we felt comfortable and free of judgment.

Shifting the burden from family history to parenting, Scott

presented a possible theory to Dr. Altman. He expressed how he'd noticed that Kelly seemed to get progressively worse when I had gone back to work full time six months earlier. He suspected that her outbursts stemmed from emotional trauma, feeling left at home by her mom. He also wondered if she may have been responding to my increased stress.

That was the first I'd heard his hypothesis. My immediate reaction centered in my gut, like I was punched with betrayal and blame. I cupped my hands, squeezing and rubbing them together, trying to keep myself from saying something I'd only regret later. *Did he really believe that her explosive tantrums, her insomnia, the constant agitation, the hitting, screaming, and banging her head on the floor were all my fault? Why hadn't we talked about this at home?*

Not wanting to appear crazy or to upset Kelly, I sucked in my darting, fearful thoughts and drew on logic to respond.

"I don't think that's the root of the problem here. Lots of moms go back to work and their kids are fine in daycare or with a babysitter." I wasn't able to see that perhaps the change had affected Kelly, even if it wasn't the source of her problems.

What were we doing playing the blame game, alluding to genetics, and pointing fingers? We were solving precisely zero of Kelly's issues, and it felt ridiculous. This meeting was for and about Kelly, to help and heal her, and we were focusing on all the wrong things, clouded by the stress of the situation. Neither of us sought to blame the other, but the fear in not knowing was bringing something ugly to the surface. The truth was that either one of us would have willingly taken a blow for her, but we needed someone else to shed light on the situation. We were both scared and blindly reaching for answers.

Dr. Altman gracefully and diplomatically shifted her attention back and forth between the two of us, giving us each a chance to share our perspective. It felt like she was trying to paint a picture rather than put together a puzzle. She didn't offer any evaluations or opinions at this point. It was clear that she wanted to gather all the facts and data before giving any recommendation or diagnosis. That felt reasonable, even preferable to me.

Handing us a stack of papers, Dr. Altman explained her plan of action. We had homework—questionnaires to fill out and pass along to Kelly's teachers to complete. Meanwhile, Dr. Altman planned to visit Kelly at Montessori to observe her in social settings. Then we would meet again to go over her findings without Kelly present.

Before ending the appointment, Dr. Altman walked over to the spot in her office where Kelly was playing and sat on the floor next to her. Then she picked up one of the figurines and pretended it was talking to the one Kelly had in her hand. Dr. Altman laughed a quirky sort of laugh that might normally be annoying, but on that particular day, it was distracting in a good way. Kelly didn't flinch, she just kept playing out the character of her figurine.

"Would it be all right with you if I visit you at school?" Dr. Altman asked Kelly.

Kelly looked at her a little confused but agreed, "Sure," and they played for a few fleeting but memorable moments.

Scott and I walked out of the office in silence, still a bit in shock from the intensity of the meeting. Kelly was happily in tow having enjoyed her playtime alone and with Dr. Altman. By the time we were in the car, I had to get it off my chest, even if my doing so would upset Kelly.

"What was that in there?" I started. "Do you really think my going back to work caused her to be like this?" His eyes focused on the road while he let me get it all out. "What were you saying exactly? The last thing I'd try to do is escape the responsibilities of being a mother by working. You do know that, right?"

He started to say something then paused, breathed deeply, and replied, "I didn't mean to blame you. Like you, I'm just trying to figure this thing out." His eyes softened with a watery glaze, and he reached over to the passenger seat where I was sitting and placed his hand on mine.

Deep down, I knew that we were on the same team, Kelly's team. We both wanted the same thing—to figure out what was going on in Kelly's body and to get her to feel good again. We just forgot, momentarily, that being fair to one another and avoiding blame needed to be part of the journey. Bending for each other, sacrificing our own egos for the greater good and the good of Kelly's health, would make us stronger together, as partners. That day, we learned that much.

About a month after our first appointment, Scott and I met again with Dr. Altman. It was the moment we'd been waiting for, and we were bracing ourselves for a diagnosis. We were hoping for a plan. Whatever it was, we thought we were ready.

We sat on the same black leather couch, each on our own side again, while Dr. Altman described what happened when she observed Kelly in school. She watched how Kelly interacted with the other kids and how Kelly responded to the teachers' direction. She walked us through everything she saw, all the signs and signals she picked up on, all the "observational data" that she gathered on Kelly.

"I believe," Dr. Altman started, "that Kelly has something called pervasive developmental disorder or PDD." She paused, giving us time to process. "It's a mild form of autism, and Kelly's case is extremely mild."

What the heck does that mean? And, what is autism anyway? Scott and I both looked away from Dr. Altman, staring off in different directions, stunned in our own private, confused worlds. Neither Scott nor I had ever even heard the word *autism* before.

There we were, finally receiving a diagnosis, the thing we'd been waiting for, and it was staggering. Neither of us could grasp the scope of Dr. Altman's words, what they meant for us, for Kelly, for our future, for today or tomorrow. We were just silent, sitting there.

Dr. Altman broke into our bewildered trance, reassuring us Kelly would be fine. Clearly, she'd had similar reactions in the past. "All this really means is that Kelly will be different, eccentric. She'll be the kind of person who will take her dog to work with her."

Then Dr. Altman advised a next step. She wrote down the name of a referral, a neuropsychologist, Dr. Martin. He would be able to give us more specifics and suggestions for treatment, recommended therapies. We both nodded as if we understood what she was talking about, but neither of us had a clue.

We thanked Dr. Altman for her careful investigation, and as we walked out of her office, it felt like trying to wade through deep water—slow, heavy steps, none without extra effort. On the way home together, we recounted the conversation, acknowledged that we both needed time to process, and agreed to wait before telling Kelly.

That night, while I prepared dinner, it was as if nothing had changed. Kelly, irritated, came over to me as I stirred the noodles in the boiling water. She asked me why I was angry. Those damn deep crevices between my eyebrows. I could feel them deepening, and it made me powerless in Kelly's presence. I couldn't relax them. I couldn't rest my face.

"You stupid!" Kelly protested when Scott tried convincing her to eat the chicken on her plate. At least now we had a reason for why she acted this way. Maybe nothing would ever be the same. Maybe this would become our normal life.

After dinner, Scott went in the basement to watch a movie with Natalie and Kelly.

"I'll be right down," I said while finishing the dishes.

Instead, I went up to my room and hid in my closet. I sat on the floor with my knees scrunched up to my chest and my arms hugging them tight. Head bowed, the tears began streaming down my cheeks and then quickly turned into heavy sobs. I was blubbering uncontrollable tears like a baby. The palms of my hands pushed deep into my eyebrows as darkness consumed me. I was surrounded by the black abyss of hanging blouses, dresses, and pants. My arms and legs were shaking lightly, a low vibration that hummed from my core. My body began to rock back and forth just like Kelly did in the car. As I sat on the carpet with all the lights off, I surrendered to just emptying everything that was inside. Finally, I'd found a place to be alone. Like a steady, hard rain, the tears wouldn't stop.

4

a whole new world

"Things you want to happen will only happen if you work really hard to make them happen."

At thirty-three years old, I decided I didn't want to have any more children.

"I want to get my tubes tied," I declared to Scott one night after dinner.

"Really?" Scott quizzically responded, pausing before continuing: "Are you sure?"

"Yes, I'm sure. I can't have any more kids. I'm done."

"Really?" he asked again either in disbelief or disagreement.

"There is no way I could take care of a baby with the way Kelly acts all day long and during the night." Exhausted, I professed my limitations, my mind already made up. "When would I sleep? Besides, I feel like I barely have any time for Natalie as it is."

"Well, I guess I could look into a vasectomy," Scott graciously offered, hesitating before completing his sentence.

"That's okay. Really, I've got no problem doing it. I'm sure," I confidently answered, wanting to get it taken care of as soon as possible.

Lying on the gurney in the hallway outside the operating room, my gynecologist leaned over me as if to tell me a secret. Through her thick framed glasses, her eyes focused on mine while her black chin-length hair fell into her face.

"Are you sure you want to do this?" she checked in with me.

After delivering both of my babies and having intimate conversations around conception, we'd bonded. She acted more like a sister or a friend than a doctor.

"Yes. I'm sure," I murmured, half loopy from the drugs they'd already given me. "I can't handle having any more children," I paused. "You remember Kelly, our second daughter? She was just diagnosed with pervasive developmental disorder." I hadn't planned to share that with her in the moment. A few tears fell down the side of my cheek and into my ear.

"You have to talk to Mary Barbera, my neighbor," she offered, always quick and willing to volunteer ideas and solutions. "Mary's son has autism, and she started the Berks Autism Society. Mary is a wealth of information." She wrote Mary's name and number on a piece of paper and handed it to the nurse to give to me after my procedure. Then, her hand cupped my shoulder and she pleaded, "Call her."

A few weeks later, I followed up and called Mary. Mary's voice was friendly, bubbling with energy and eager to help. She invited me over to her house. When Mary opened her front door, she greeted me with a pleasant but sympathetic look, as if she was welcoming me to the club. After a quick and proper introduction, we headed straight into her family room where we spent the next two hours on her couch talking. At one point during the conversation, I glanced up and noticed that her dining room table was completely covered with stacks of books, presumably all on autism. This was going to be a new way of life. If I was going to help Kelly, I needed to understand that.

Overwhelmed by the newness of it all—the therapy, the theories and the treatments—I listened intently to everything Mary told me. Even though I was in unfamiliar territory, I told her I wanted to hear it all. She was a combination of teacher, friend, and coach, instructing me on all the steps I needed to take for Kelly.

Mary did her best to explain the process of behavior therapy and specifically what they were doing with her son—applied behavior analysis or ABA. She told me that ABA was the only behavior therapy with proven results. Lucas, her son, was nonverbal. On a TV monitor, we watched as the therapist worked with him. He was so different from Kelly—you'd never know they both had autism. Mary recommended I reach out to another mom with a child on the higher-functioning end of the autistic spectrum and gave me a list of names and phone numbers.

Leaving her house, my hands fumbled to hold the stack of books and pamphlets that explained all the therapies and listed therapist names for behavior, speech, and sensory issues. Back then, the internet and Google weren't readily accessible, which made her knowledge and advice all the more valuable.

There was no one focused resource for all the tools, therapies, or discussions around autism. I bought a binder and started writing notes. On one page, I wrote all the references Mary recommended and on another, I made a list of all the behaviors I wanted to target with Kelly. New terms, studies, and proven therapies started to weave a web of understanding in my mind where there was once a dark, hollow space. It felt like learning a foreign language. Canals were being dug where my fears had been building fortresses.

Soon after talking with Mary, I met with a local wraparound agency regarding ABA therapy. At this point, what I understood was that wraparound services consisted of a team of therapists led by a behavioral specialist with a master's in counseling who would oversee an individualized plan for Kelly. The therapists or TSS—short for therapeutic support staff—would come into our home to work with Kelly, shadow her at school, and as a team, we would develop and implement goals for Kelly. The agency had a crew in mind for Kelly, but unfortunately said it would be a few months before there was an opening.

A couple weeks later, Mary called me to ask if I'd want to go with her to a conference on the newest studies and practices concerning ABA. A world-renowned autism expert, Dr. O. Ivar Lovaas, was hosting the conference.

"Sure!" I said, excited to gain a greater understanding of this therapy and to spend more time learning from Mary.

The conference was in Staten Island. I asked Scott to come with me, to spend a day off together, educating ourselves on our challenging new endeavor with Kelly. Our babysitter would take care of getting the girls to school, picking them up, and staying with them until we got home that evening. Scott and I left early that morning to get there by the time the conference started at nine a.m. We met Mary there. She'd driven separately with another friend. The four of us sat side-by-side in the large auditorium.

During the entire conference, Scott and I took notes voraciously like two nervous students in their first college class, trying to keep up with all the stats and facts they hadn't heard before and never wanted to forget. When we got home that night, after the girls were in bed, we compared notes. This was the first time the two of us had a focused conversation about Kelly's therapy, about why it was so important, and why it consumed me. While I knew in my heart Scott supported me—often in a silent, accepting way—Scott's interaction with me that day was the burst of active participation and validation that I needed from him.

"Thank you for coming. It meant a lot to have you there," I said to Scott, then kissed his lips gently before dozing off to sleep.

The conference set the tone for this new phase we were about to enter. It motivated me to get things moving. Lovaas taught us that the earlier the intervention, the better. In the weeks that followed, I focused every free moment on research and arranging all of Kelly's therapies. Through two local hospitals, I found a speech therapist and an occupational therapist. There was a two-month waiting list for speech therapy, but fortunately Kelly could start occupational therapy right away.

So, in November of 2000, when Kelly was four years old, we were introduced to occupational therapy. Based on her assessment, Kelly would go three times a week. The goal, her therapist told us, was to work on both fine and gross motor skills while also addressing her sensory issues.

In one of Kelly's first sessions, Judy, the therapist, played a beanbag toss game with Kelly. With encouraging words and a soft lighthearted laugh, Judy tried cheering Kelly on, but Kelly's malevolent glare told me she was not amused or enjoying the game. Kelly stared downward, squeezed her lips together, and clenched her arms at her sides. Frowning, Kelly leaned into me and hissed, "Mom, tell her not to laugh!"

Then, Kelly sat back down on the spot where Judy had asked her to sit, a distance of maybe four feet from the wooden board with the round cutout target holes. But instead of throwing the bags, Kelly scooted her bottom right in front of the board and deliberately placed the beanbags in the holes. It was obvious she didn't like the rules and wanted to ensure her success. Afterward, Kelly smiled while her gaze turned away from Judy, and then Kelly proceeded to neatly stack the bags in a pile on the other side of the wooden board.

Instead of harping on Kelly for cheating, Judy pointed out to me how Kelly preferred to sit on her knees with her feet tucked under her bottom, noting that it would make Kelly's hamstrings tight.

"Work on getting her to sit cross legged," Judy advised.

Like that's a priority, I thought, knowing we had much bigger fish to fry. I left that first session unsure what to think, but made a conscious promise to myself to stay committed and calm.

It was hard to stay cool and collected at home. At night, by the time Scott returned from work, he and I barely had the chance to talk. Kelly interrupted our conversations constantly, inevitably. When Scott was fed up with it, he reprimanded her with the noble intention of trying to teach her right and wrong.

"You're ruining our night," he told her.

"You're ruining my life!" Kelly snarled back at him, echoing his words with dark, squinted eyes. Scott jerked his head back and opened his mouth, but resisted another useless reprimand.

Kelly's demands were relentless and persistent. Unconsciously and impulsively, I would respond to her as if she was still a crying baby. I was so shaken by her angry outbursts that it was hard for me to shift gears and carry a normal conversation with anyone, even Natalie, even my own husband. Kelly's behaviors were becoming so unpredictably out of control that I'd also given up on using babysitters.

There was no choice. We'd come to the conclusion that I had to quit working. It was too stressful to juggle work along with needing to be Kelly's caregiver around the clock, managing her therapy, trying to constantly smooth things over, and keep order in the house. These were each full-time jobs that I'd have to do on my own. Maybe I wasn't good at asking for help. Maybe I was better at internalizing everything, pushing frustration down, swallowing screams and tears deeper. Maybe it was all I knew how to do to get from morning to night.

When he was home, Scott took on the role of protector. He was trying to cushion Natalie and me from Kelly's relentless, mindless abuse, but it wasn't helping on any front. Without knowing, his approach was instigating more outrage in Kelly. He'd interrupt her ranting with reprimands like "No yelling, Kelly!" or "Yelling makes Mommy mad. Stop yelling!"

With his voice, deep and loud, Scott tried to scare Kelly into behaving more like Natalie. She wasn't Natalie: that, we knew. I'd cringe when he'd respond to her like this. *Of course it doesn't work*, I wanted to shout. *Kelly is different!* I wanted to jump in, but more often than not, I chose silence. The house was already up in arms. Natalie had already left the room. This was our world. This would continue until bedtime—Kelly crying inconsolably, thrashing her arms and legs as she rolled around on the floor.

"I hate the music." Kelly banged her head on the floor when the radio played jazz in the background. On rainy days, it was "I hate the weather!" Most days, in a loud, irritated voice, out of nowhere, she'd yell, "I hate you, Mommy."

At night, before bed, I'd run her a bath thinking it would pacify her. From the bathroom, I could hear her screaming that she couldn't get her clothes off. "My clothes are taped on me!" she'd yell. When I walked in, I found her hitting her thighs with her fists in frustration. Once in the hot water, Kelly relaxed a bit, giving me a short reprieve before moving into the dreaded bedtime routine.

Kelly loved bedtime stories but had a hard time sitting still and often acted them out with her toys or props. Then, when it was time to say goodnight, she didn't want to stop playing or to lie in bed by herself. Scott and I took turns between her and Natalie. When it was my turn with Kelly, Scott often had to step in to help me pry the toys from her hands and then he would hold her tight so her arms couldn't grab, hit, or thrash in protest.

Once we said goodnight and left her in her room, Kelly started her bedtime yelling ritual: "I want Mommy!"

When we tried ignoring her, I'd hear Natalie go into Kelly's room and nicely tell her, "If you want Mommy, go to the kitchen."

Kelly would run downstairs into the kitchen and back into the hall again, screaming, "Stop it! I want Mommy. I want Mommy!" While hitting her head repetitively with her hand, she hollered, "I hate my brain!" Then she demanded, "No one is ever going up to my room again!"

Sometimes I'd simply give up on interpreting what she was trying to tell me. It was easier to just let it go. Instead of responding with words or reprimands, I'd stand by her, listen, and hope she'd calm down on her own. Over and over in my head, I convinced myself that her nonsensical screams were merely pleas for understanding, healing and love, so that was what I tried to give her. Once she succumbed to bed, I'd collapse into my own bed, praying for sleep.

5

tummy troubles

"Never let doubt fill your mind. Instead, let hope fill your mind."

Potty-training Kelly was a never-ending nightmare—sort of like a high-pitched ringing that, after days and weeks of pulsating without pause, simply fades into the background. Sure, you're conditioned to the sound, but it's still there, scraping away at your patience and sanity.

Even though we started when she turned two years old, Kelly wasn't fully trained until she was three. Just like her aversion to people's expressions, if the toilet didn't look right to her in that moment, she wouldn't go. Coaching her gently, I'd watch her stare into the water. I guessed that she was afraid of the dark hole at the bottom of the toilet bowl—another strange phobia we could never understand. *Does she imagine getting sucked in? Does she think a ferocious monster will jump out of the water?*

At times, I thought that maybe Kelly just felt the need to reject anything and everything I asked of her. Maybe she didn't like when I spoke calmly. I was at a loss. Whatever it was, she couldn't find the words to explain it. Though there were many battles, I knew she was fighting with the fear, not with me.

In the summer of 2000, a few months after Dr. Altman's autism diagnosis, we were on vacation in Nantucket with my family. It was a beautiful, sunny summer day, and I was in the kitchen making lunch to take to the beach. My younger sister, Cindy, came in and grabbed my arm gently, turning me toward her. She looked me in the eye, leaning in to get closer to me as if she had something important and top secret to tell me. A grimace of disgust was smeared across her face.

In a quiet but roused tone, Cindy told me that she went into the powder room right after Kelly and that Kelly hadn't flushed the toilet. *I know. She never does. Big deal!* I thought to myself.

Still frowning with disbelief, my sister whispered to me, "Do her poops always look like that?"

I had no idea what she meant. Feeling like she was judging Kelly and me, I answered honestly with as few words as possible, "I don't know." Then I left the kitchen and walked toward the bathroom to investigate. Sitting on the edge of the white porcelain toilet bowl, where there was no water, was a huge, very mushy pile of tannish, mustard yellow colored feces. Frankly, I was relieved Kelly was finally using the toilet independently and hadn't paid much attention to the color or consistency of her bowel movements. The tantrums, the little to no sleep, the hyperactivity, and the lack of focus all still consumed every drop of my attention and energy.

"No, that's not usual. It must be from the orange juice she just drank." I made something up to ease my sister's mind and then forgot about it.

I didn't think about Kelly's bowels again until four months later on Christmas Eve. I remember the day perfectly, and it had nothing to do with Santa Claus, yuletide carols, or holiday spirit. Kelly was four years old and Natalie was six. In our classic Christmas Eve tradition, we planned to go to church for an early family service and then to my parents' house for dinner.

The girls reveled in this tradition because their grandparents' house sparkled and glowed with Christmas spirit. My dad loved everything about Christmas—decorating the tree, giving gifts, singing carols, and carving the honorary turkey. Over the past few years, at a local antique flea market, he'd garnered a collection of vintage Santa figurines of all different shapes, sizes, expressions, and shades of red. Proudly, he propped them up in clusters on a long wooden bench in the brick vestibule outside the front door of my parents' house. The Santas greeted us at the door, their painted expressions whispering promises of Christmas magic. A few had dark, distant eyes, solemn grins; others had hard plastic faces and worn, velveteen bodies. Something about them gave me pause—like that feeling when your unconscious mind is warning you of trouble but you don't know what it is yet.

This year, my mom bought Christmas dresses for my girls. The dresses were fancier than anything they had ever worn. The skirts of the dresses were made of several layers of tulle like a beautiful ballerina costume. From the waist up, the material was a soft, smooth velvet. A matching tulle bow tied at the back of the waist, separating the skirt from the velvet top. Natalie's dress was dark emerald green and Kelly's was a rich maroon that was more purple than red. Both girls were waiting for the hour that they could dress up like little princesses. First, though, we had to sleep through the night.

Around two o'clock in the morning on Christmas Eve, Kelly's pointer finger gently poked my shoulder.

"Mom," she whispered in an apologetic tone. "I went diarrhea."

Grunting, I peeled myself out of bed and mumbled, "Okay, I'm coming."

I don't know why I was surprised. It was so predictable. Every Thanksgiving or Christmas, one or both of the girls got sick. This time, it appeared to be a simple, seasonal stomach virus that lasted all night. By morning, Kelly couldn't keep anything in her little belly. Even a few sips of water sent her running to the potty. Despite the fact that she was obviously sick, Kelly was smiling and oozing with energy from the excitement of the events to come that night. She wasn't worried. It was as if she pretended that the virus didn't exist or that it would magically go away, but I knew better.

How could I possibly tell Kelly she couldn't wear her fancy dress or that we aren't going to Mom-Mom and JoJo's for Christmas Eve? I would have to dream up another plan, explain that we would have to find another way to celebrate. But how? There was no way she would understand or accept that decision.

All I could do was imagine the horror of a runny mess uncontrollably seeping out from under her beautiful dress onto my mom's custom-designed upholstered furniture. And what about Natalie? Just because Kelly was sick, would Natalie have to miss out on all the fun too? Reluctantly, I called my mom and let her know, telling her that if things were really bad that we might not make it.

Worried that Kelly was going to get dehydrated, I gave her a popsicle. Two bites and an explosive diarrhea bomb sent her running to the bathroom. Though I thought it was merely a nasty virus and would eventually go away, I wanted Kelly to see a doctor, hoping maybe they'd have some solution we hadn't thought of yet.

Since it was a holiday, all four of us—Scott, Natalie, Kelly and I—piled into our maroon Toyota Sienna minivan to go the doctor. It was our first visit to this pediatrician's practice. Upon arriving, the nurse at the front desk reminded us that Natalie and Kelly were "accepted" as new patients, gave me some paperwork to fill out, and informed us that the girls were assigned a young female doctor. For this appointment, however, we were going to see the founder and most respected doctor in the practice, Dr. Adams.

"Hi, I'm Dr. Adams," he said, introducing himself as he walked into the exam room where all four of us were sitting, waiting. Dr. Adams wore a brown-and-white plaid button-down shirt and a beige cardigan sweater. His mousy brown hair was brushed back to one side. He had a pointy nose, dark beady eyes, and a quiet but quirky voice. Dr. Adams reminded me of Mr. Rogers.

Like Mr. Rogers, Dr. Adams spoke in a methodical, slow pace.

As he began asking Kelly questions, his patient, gentle, and engaging approach built trust in her. He was speaking her language and she was responding with ease. Some of my friends referred to Dr. Adams as a "child whisperer" because he intuitively knew what made kids tick—he saw right to the core of their personalities and made quick, accurate diagnoses.

I was curious if he knew from reading our application that Kelly had a mild form of autism, but decided not to bring it up. Kelly pretended like nothing was wrong and smiled at Dr. Adams with her hands in her lap and legs crossed while she sat up on the exam table. I tried not to show my delight in her behavior for fear that it'd send her in the other direction. Natalie was perfectly composed by her side, as always. Despite the fact that Kelly kept skipping out the door to go to the bathroom, she was trying hard to be on her best behavior for Christmas Eve.

It was as if her spirit was bigger than her body, trying with all its might to draw on its own healing energy, grasping for control over this stomach bug that was interrupting her fun. Kelly and her spirit were working in tandem, fighting to make her better in time for Santa.

Dr. Adams didn't take his eyes off Kelly while he spoke to me and Scott. It was as if he and Kelly had an unspoken conversation, and he watched her every move. In his head, he counted that she went to the bathroom seventeen times during the short period we were in the exam room. When he shared that with us, he immediately followed it with his diagnosis. Kelly had the rotavirus. When he recommended that she be admitted to the hospital, he whispered the bad news to us, so as not to freak Kelly out.

"Since it is Christmas Eve and I can see she's a fighter, I will leave it up to you."

Having never met Kelly before, it was shocking how Dr. Adams translated her symptoms and immediately perceived her resilience, quickly labeling her a fighter. Because Kelly usually stuck to her own agenda and did not listen well or follow the rules, most people, including her grandparents, the old pediatrician, and many of her teachers, labeled Kelly as either stubborn or spoiled. Dr. Adams saw that there was more to her than that. When I looked in his eyes, I could see the wheels spinning inside his head, exploring the same questions I had been asking myself for so many months: *What is taking control of my beautiful, blonde, blue-eyed angel? Where is my happy little girl?*

Dr. Adams gave us very specific instructions. We were to give Kelly tiny amounts of liquids on a systematic schedule to keep her from dehydrating.

"Call if you change your minds. Remember, the IV fluids would make her better much faster," were his parting words.

It was still morning so we had some time. By early afternoon, Scott and I decided we wouldn't make it to church but still planned to go to my parents'. I held my breath hoping Kelly would get through the next few hours without an accident.

Like a Christmas miracle, it came true. At my parents' house, there were presents to distract Kelly from the fact that she couldn't eat the turkey, mashed potatoes, or colorfully decorated star shaped cut-out cookies. Motivated by Santa coming down the chimney, Kelly made it through Christmas Eve and Christmas without getting dehydrated.

Two weeks later, Kelly still had diarrhea and tummy aches, even on the BRAT diet of bland, boring foods like bananas, rice, applesauce, and toast.

"I think we need to go back to Dr. Adams," I conferred with Scott. He agreed. He, too, had an inkling that this was about something more than just a stomach virus. When I called Dr. Adams' office and explained the situation, the nurse acknowledged the abnormality and said Dr. Adams could see us the next day. Grateful, I looked forward to an insightful discussion with him.

As Kelly and I walked down the narrow carpeted hallway to

Dr. Adams' office, Kelly kept turning around to look at her shadow—
something she'd recently started doing. I wondered if I should
share this new information with the doctor. I didn't know what
was normal or abnormal anymore.

Inside the exam room, Dr. Adams' gaze was fixed on Kelly
again, carefully observing her in her realm over in the corner.

"I'm afraid there's something more going on here. This is out
of my scope of practice." He conceded with a sigh. "I'm going to
refer you to a pediatric gastroenterologist." And he wrote down
the name.

In February, we went to a satellite office of Children's Hospital
of Philadelphia (CHOP) to see the specialist, Dr. Johnson. After a
forty-minute drive, anxious for some answers, I waited with Kelly
in the exam room until the doctor came in and introduced himself.
This doctor was very different from Dr. Adams in both his mannerisms and approach. He was expressionless as if his attention was
elsewhere and didn't talk to Kelly at all. While he listened to me
describe Kelly's history of symptoms, his compressed lips and nar-
rowing eyes hinted that he'd already come to his own conclusion.
His diagnosis was that it was still the rotavirus making her sick.

"If she doesn't improve after a few more weeks, call the office
for another appointment," he advised while shaking my hand and
walking out the door. No tests, no medicine, just a wait and see approach. I took a deep breath and gulped, swallowing my questions.

On the drive back home, a heavy tightness settled into my
shoulders and chest. I felt dismissed, disappointed, and discouraged. Though I hated the idea, I was already convinced this was
more than just the rotavirus. Yet, I still had no answers or explanations as to why Kelly was sick for over a month now. Anxiety manifested itself in a painful acidic stomach. It was no coincidence that
I was starting to think that Kelly's stomach issues would never go
away. On the way home, I called Scott and vented my frustration.

"Let's wait and see. I'm sure there's an answer," Scott said, his deep, velvety voice soothing my fears and reminding me that he was by my side, even when he wasn't. Together we'd get to the bottom of this.

In the weeks that followed, we were in constant fluctuation between bellyaches, vomiting, and insomnia. Kelly cried while wrapping her arms around her waist, throwing herself on the floor and into the fetal position. This happened almost every day. In the middle of the night, she'd explode in the bathroom with uncontrollable episodes of diarrhea or vomiting. If she wasn't awake because she was sick, then it was insomnia. I couldn't understand how her little body didn't sleep. *Doesn't she need sleep? I need sleep!*

Every night, I'd wake to the sound of a light tapping noise from her fist softly knocking on our bedroom door or her little pointer finger gently poking my shoulder. I knew she didn't want to be awake. It wasn't her fault. Maybe she was having nightmares, maybe she was scared of the dark—I could only guess why she was afraid to close her eyes. She wasn't telling me with words.

"Why can't you sleep?" I'd ask.

Kelly grabbed her hair, pulling on it as she looked at the floor.

"I don't know," she said, shrugging.

"Come on, let's go to sleep. It's nighttime sweetie, everyone needs to sleep," I'd tell her.

No sooner did I crawl back under my cozy down comforter, close my eyes, and doze off when I'd feel the gentle breeze of Kelly's breath and the tip of her finger poking me again. She wanted me, always jabbing my shoulder, not Scott's. Delirious from exhaustion, after Kelly made two or three visits to our bedroom, my patience was depleted. Fatigued and frustrated, I'd take it out on Kelly, yelling from under the covers.

"Go back to bed, Kelly! I'm tired. I need to sleep!"

Once my voice raised, Scott chimed in too: "Go back to bed, Kelly," he'd groggily growl at her. But yelling, his or mine, did nothing. Besides, yelling—whether I delivered or received it—never felt good to me. So, as usual, I'd continue to crawl out of bed and begrudgingly redirect her back to her room.

Scott suggested she climb in bed with us, but I didn't want to open that can of worms. Our king-sized bed, as large as it was, was still a sacred place for just us, husband and wife. It was the only time I could count on us being alone together. Besides, I guessed that even if we did let Kelly come in our bed, she still wouldn't be able to sleep. This was not separation anxiety. It was something much worse.

Natalie and Kelly shared a bathroom. It was renovated before we moved in—the entire mold-infested floor and shower had been gutted, and the tub, sink, and toilet all replaced. I wanted the girls, and our guests, to feel clean and fresh when they were in their bathroom. I loved the wallpaper we hung on the walls. It was a black and white French toile pattern that my mother had used in her house in Nantucket. The girls' bathroom was just the right size for the leftover rolls of wallpaper. The snowy-white floor was a one-inch hexagon tile with a matte finish that surrounded the brand new white porcelain pedestal sink and toilet.

Kelly's nightly torment often involved diarrhea or vomit which, of course, required a lot of cleaning up and disinfecting. Standing there, in the middle of the night, wiping up splattered feces from the white tile, wallpaper, and toilet depressed and exhausted me. When Natalie woke up in the morning and walked in the bathroom, I didn't want her to have to imagine how her sister just threw up all over it, to see evidence of diarrhea on the walls, or to smell the remnants of the stinky stool or vomit lingering in the air. Just thinking about how to make it all right again would make me cry helpless tears in those delirious, dark moments.

Of course, that wasn't it. There were also the sheets on Kelly's bed. They had to be carried down to the basement to be put in the washing machine along with the towels used to clean up the mess. During those early morning hours, Scott and I were a team. He'd take care of the dirty sheets and towels while I dealt with Kelly. The carpet had to be sprayed with Resolve to remove the drips and leaks that uncontrollably escaped from her bottom as she walked from her room to the bathroom, which Scott also cleaned up.

And Kelly, covered in the mess of the night, needed washing too. So there I sat, at odd hours of the early morning, giving her a bath. Even when all the cleaning up was done, I still felt like everything was filthy, and it was. Everything was covered in filth. This was just not normal. *Who else lives like this?*

One night, I peeled myself out of bed to walk Kelly back to her room. Luckily, this time she wasn't sick; she just couldn't sleep. When we reached her doorway, my drowsy eyes were blinded by the brightness. With all her lights on, she'd been busy. There was an elaborate display of Barbie dolls laying across the light-blue carpet of her floor. The dolls were lined up in rows. Little pillows were under each of their heads with blankets over their bodies, all made of toilet paper.

After weeks of this nocturnal routine, Dr. Johnson prescribed Zantac to help with sleep and hopefully remedy Kelly's nausea. It was hard for me to believe that my four-year-old had acid reflux, so I asked Dr. Johnson if there was any chance that Kelly's symptoms were the result of a food allergy.

"No," he said, quickly dismissing me. "Allergies are present from birth. If this was an allergy, you would have known it long ago."

So, we were back on our own again, trial and error. Night waking, bouts of diarrhea, vomiting, scrubbing, repeat. In the midst of the blurry exhaustion, there were very few good days. Yet, somehow, Kelly still showed us sparks of her playful, imaginative spirit here and there throughout the week. During these moments, I'd find her in the basement playroom, dressing up in her Mary Poppins outfit—a flowy white satin dress-up skirt that almost reached the floor, a blue plaid cotton scarf around her neck, a smashed black straw hat on her head, blue satin gloves on her tiny hands, and a shiny black patent leather pocket book over her arm. As she watched the Mary Poppins movie, Kelly sang and danced in front of the television along with Julie Andrews.

"Let's go fly a kite, up to the highest height, and send it soaring," Kelly sang along, rocking back and forth from one foot to the other, grinning whenever she'd pause or return to simply watching the movie. Sometimes I thought Kelly believed that she was in the movie in the same way that Michael, Jane, and Mary Poppins jump through the chalkboard drawing into the fantasy world of the carousel, race horses, and dancing penguins.

Whenever he could, on weekends and some weeknights, Scott would sit down with the girls and watch musicals with them. Mary Poppins was a favorite. He'd pretend to be Bert while Kelly was Mary Poppins. They'd sing along together and soon "Let's Go Fly a Kite" became his and Kelly's song. They'd belt it out together even when the movie wasn't playing. He often used the song to lift her spirits when he sensed a tantrum or protest brewing.

Music soothed Kelly's soul. She was happiest when she was watching a musical. Despite all the pain we witnessed her suffer through, Kelly still showed us glimmers of her contagious happy spirit. It was hidden inside her somewhere, underneath all the mess. Knowing it was there helped me forgive all the sleepless nights and her uncontrollable, agitated, and ornery behaviors.

Then, one brisk and sunny day in late February, I woke up and realized that Kelly hadn't come poking my shoulder during the early morning hours. Instead of waking me up repeatedly, maybe five consecutive times, between one and four in the morning, she let me sleep. Kelly let me start my morning routine and didn't bug Natalie who was getting ready for school. While Kelly slept, I ate breakfast, quickly dropped Natalie off at the bus stop down the street, came home, sipped two cups of tea, and ran a couple loads of laundry. I tried to remember the last time our house was this peaceful, quiet. I conceded to let her sleep, school could wait.

Besides, it was only preschool. I called to tell them she'd either be late or miss the day. My breath was steady and slow and my body relaxed in the silence.

Around ten o'clock in the morning, I decided I'd better wake Kelly. Gently, I pushed open the heavy wood door to her room and tiptoed along the creaky floor to the edge of her bed. I stood over her in a rare moment, watching her sleeping little figure, so limp and serene. Not even the aura of my body standing above her roused her. She appeared to be still deep in sleep. But, no, I retracted. Kelly was so sensitive to noise, something had to be wrong. Suddenly, gratitude shifted to panic.

I reached out and gently touched her forehead with the back of my hand. It didn't seem as though she had a fever, but sounded like she was breathing heavier than normal. She wasn't struggling, but the air passed slower and louder in and out of her nostrils as I watched her chest rise and fall in a perfect rhythm. Even though everything appeared fine, I had a bad feeling. She seemed perfectly healthy the day before—no sniffles, no cough, no earache or sore throat. But I still felt like something was wrong.

I went to my room, called Dr. Adams' office, and explained what I saw. The nurse said to bring Kelly in right away. I lifted her from her bed, carried her downstairs and into the car. She was in and out of consciousness. My heart was racing, but I was on auto-pilot. Keys in the ignition, reverse, left, right to the second light. Red lights were taking forever to turn green, and the car in front of me was driving torturously slow. When we got there, a nurse took me right back to an exam room. As I walked through the hallway carrying Kelly, still in her pajamas, she lifted her heavy head and vomit projected all over both of us, dripping onto the floor. Finally, her eyes were open, but she was drowsy and now whimpering with confusion. Suddenly, I thought I had nothing to worry about.

"Looks like just another virus, right?" I said to the nurse, re-lieved. She handed me paper towels to wipe up the vomit while

Kelly's lifeless, limp body was still in my arms.

"Let's see what the doctor says. I'll get some more paper towels," she offered, smiling. I recognized that smile—a caring face that didn't know how else to help.

The doctor examined Kelly carefully, and I could tell she wasn't writing this off as quickly as I had. Kelly couldn't sit up on the table so I stood next to her, holding her as the doctor placed her stethoscope on Kelly's back and listened to her breathing.

"She has pneumonia."

To be sure, the doctor ordered an X-ray. Yep, a full-blown case of pneumonia. Despite Kelly's fragile stomach, the doctor assured me that antibiotics were the necessary treatment. Sure enough, within a few days on the antibiotic, Kelly was back to her normal self.

At this point, Kelly was still taking Zantac, which seemed to be helping. But, even though they were less frequent, Kelly continued to have episodes of stomach pain, diarrhea, and vomiting, almost always in the middle of the night. So, in June, a month after Kelly turned five, and six months after all her tummy troubles began, Dr. Johnson recommended an endoscopy and colonoscopy.

"That way we can really see what's going on inside her gut," he assured.

As I thought about a tube going down Kelly's throat and up her bottom, I became queasy. Saliva backed up in my mouth as I tried to swallow. I don't know if I was more nervous about the anesthesia and procedures or the possibility of, after all that, still ending up without a diagnosis or treatment plan. The line between the two fears was blurred by this point. My confidence that Kelly could handle it was extremely low, but nevertheless, I reluctantly consented to the testing, convincing myself that this may be the only way to really know what was causing her symptoms to persist. Scott agreed.

On the day of the procedures, Scott took Natalie, about to

finish up first grade, to the bus stop. Meanwhile, I brought my mother along with me and Kelly for support and an extra pair of hands. Nervous, my fingers tightly clutched the steering wheel as we drove along the windy, congested Schuylkill Expressway on our way to Center City, Philadelphia. Any slight jerk, sudden stop, or swerve of the steering wheel could set Kelly off. My mom's job was to sit next to Kelly and to distract her from my stress, which she did by calmly occupying Kelly in conversation, games, and giggles the entire ride. Every time I glanced at Kelly in the rearview mirror, she was rocking back and forth with a smile on her face. Even with two days of grueling prep, Kelly couldn't grasp what was about to happen. Simply put, she just thought the doctor was taking a look inside her tummy.

Despite the stop-and-go traffic and Kelly's complaints of hunger and thirst, the three of us got through the hour-and-a-half drive. After checking in, a nurse began prepping Kelly for the procedures. When Kelly needed to go to the bathroom, the nurse accompanied her so she could get a look at Kelly's bowel movement before Kelly flushed.

"There's a lot of mucus in her stool," the nurse observed but didn't explain further. *What does that mean?* I wondered as I fiddled with my purse, trying to hide my shaking hands and quivering legs.

When it was time, I hated leaving Kelly but had no choice. My mom and I told her we'd be there waiting for her and reminded her when she was done that she could have whatever she wanted to eat.

About an hour later, as my mom and I were walking back from the hospital cafeteria and approaching the waiting room, I heard a child tearfully yelling at the top of her lungs. It was Kelly. The doctor met me outside the recovery room to report his findings while my mom offered to go try and soothe Kelly.

"She's got a bacterial infection, clostridium difficile or C. diff, esophagitis, and acid reflux."

Relieved, I placed my right hand over my mouth while taking a long, deep breath in through my nose. Then I crossed my arms over my chest and took another long, deep breath exhaling hard out of my mouth.

He continued, "The treatment is an antibiotic, Flagyl, for the bacterial infection and Prilosec for the gastritis. She also has a lactase deficiency. Give her Lactaid tablets to help break down the lactase in dairy."

"Okay, could you please say that again?" My thoughts jumbled while I struggled to write everything down.

Information. Results. One more deep breath. I was so grateful.

After two brutal days of prep, an adverse reaction to the anesthesia, and some McDonald's fries, we got back in the car. Kelly fell asleep almost immediately, her rosy cheek pressed against my mother's shoulder, blonde wisps of hair falling around her face.

"Thanks, Mom. I couldn't have done it without you."

We recounted the day and next steps while Kelly slept. Once back home, I dropped my mom off at her house while Kelly continued sleeping in the car.

A few minutes later, I carried Kelly into our house and up to her room. Gently, I covered her with a blanket, sure that she'd sleep through the afternoon. I stood at the doorway, looking back at Kelly, sleeping soundly and peacefully. If I could place my hand on her skin and have the sickness flow out of her little body into mine, I would. I promised that I would, but I couldn't. Healing was something we'd have to fight for, and Kelly and I were fighters. I don't know if I passed on the grit to her or if she taught me how to fight. I have a feeling it was a little bit of both.

6

looking for a hero

"Never look back on the past with regret because you can't change it. Look to the future and think about how you want things to be better, and they will get better."

Three days after her endoscopy and colonoscopy, Kelly had a fever. She woke up in the middle of the night vomiting. Same thing the next day.

"My tummy hurts," Kelly continued to complain at least several times a week, even after finishing the antibiotic and while still taking Prilosec. Maybe this just par for the course with a diagnosis of esophagitis and acid reflux, but I wasn't sure. When I called Dr. Johnson's office to inquire, his assistant tried reassuring me by saying Kelly's symptoms were likely just lactose intolerance. She also chalked up the nausea to being a common symptom of esophagitis.

"Give her the Prilosec twice a day and come back in three months," she told me, requesting I give it more time. But I wasn't convinced that's what Kelly needed.

By the end of summer, the spells subsided somewhat, just enough to encourage Scott and I that Kelly was ready to try to go to school. We crossed our fingers, held our breath, and sent her back to Montessori. During that initial week of school, at home alone for the first time in a long time, I called a family friend whose son was also diagnosed with PDD. If it weren't for autism, I wouldn't have reached out to her. I was searching for someone

who would understand, who would listen without judging or trying to offer pointless advice.

"How's Kelly?" Lisa asked me.

"She's still having some tummy troubles, though not as bad as
it was in the summer." I acknowledged the struggle, but tried to
downplay my frustration.

"You need to see Connor's doctor, Dr. Baker," Lisa enthusiastically suggested. "He specializes in treating kids with autism and
their gut issues."

This was the first time I'd heard anyone make the connection between autism and digestive problems, as if they went hand in hand,
as if what was happening with Kelly was not unusual. This made me
especially curious since Connor didn't have the same symptoms as
Kelly. In fact, he had no visible or notable digestive distress.

Lisa had decided to take a holistic approach that she'd learned
about from another mom with a son on the autistic spectrum.
Since she'd gotten Connor on his current routine, she'd been upbeat and had a positive outlook on Connor's progress. Lisa was,
simply put, content. She swore by Dr. Baker's influence on this
progress. As I listened to her, I was still skeptical of anything other
than standard medical practice.

"I think Kelly's stomach issues are too complex and need the
care of a specialist," I admitted, dismissing Lisa's attempt to guide
me in a different direction. Besides, I thought, Dr. Baker is in Connecticut. How would I handle driving with Kelly four hours each
way for an appointment? I thanked her for the advice, and we
changed the subject.

When I hung up the phone, I couldn't stop thinking about
Lisa and Connor. Her steadfast belief in Connor's regimen and
her satisfaction played over and over in my mind. I wanted to
feel safe and on the right track. I wanted to feel the same sense of
contentment that Lisa felt. At this point, the only plan we had was
a prescription for Prilosec.

I began considering Lisa's advice. Even if it was "holistic," an approach I'd always thought of as woo-woo medicine, the ongoing support, tweaking, tracking, and problem-solving were all very appealing at this point. It was an alternative I was ready to try. A few days later, I called her back.

As if she was waiting for my call, Lisa spewed out a litany of information, specific and general, all praising Connor's doctor. Dr. Baker was part of a growing group of doctors focused on finding treatments for kids with autism. These were mainstream doctors, mostly MDs, trained in a standard fashion. But they also shared an interest in understanding the body in a different, new way. They wanted to peel back layers, dig deeper to discover what was actually causing problems rather than simply treating the symptoms. This progressive group of doctors called themselves DAN, standing for Defeat Autism Now.

Lisa continued, almost without taking a breath. I started jotting down names and notes. DAN was started by Dr. Bernard Rimland and the Autism Research Institute in San Diego, California. Dr. Rimland was a pioneer in the world of autism research. In his revolutionary book, *Infantile Autism*, published in 1964, he debunked the conventional theory that autism was caused by a child's response to an unaffectionate, "refrigerator" mother. His passion was born out of the challenges he faced with his own son with autism. Dr. Rimland devoted his life to researching biomedical approaches for treating autism.

Lisa plowed forward. Many DAN doctors were like Dr. Rimland, she said. Having children of their own with autism, they appreciated the need for a better way. While autism was typically treated as a psychiatric disorder with behavior, speech, and occupational therapy as treatments, DAN doctors' personal crusades united them in the theory that autism involves a combination of biochemical factors such as lowered immune response, a break down in methylation, as well as environmental factors including toxins from multiple sources and food triggers. These doctors were driven by intrigue and determination to figure out the puzzle of autism.

Bottom line, Lisa declared, DAN's message was this: *These kids are sick, not crazy.* To many moms like myself, this made a lot of sense and was more aligned with what we were living with every day. For me, I felt like it was the best news I'd heard in a long time. In my gut, I knew that I hadn't lost my happy, smart little girl. Something was masking the precious human spirit inside, robbing her of her natural instinct to be happy and full of virtuous energy. Something was making it impossible for her to carry out regular, simple daily activities. Something was keeping her from eating without getting sick.

I recounted Lisa's stories and information to Scott, and we agreed the approach was worth a try. Lisa told me that there was a conference coming up, organized and hosted by DAN. That would be the perfect introduction, I thought.

A month later, in early October, Scott and I drove to Boston for the DAN Conference. The girls stayed at home with the babysitter that had known them since they were babies, the one I'd used and felt comfortable with while I was working full time. I gave her a very detailed list of Kelly's meals and routine, hoping Kelly wouldn't get sick while we were gone. Though I knew I'd be thinking about Kelly and Natalie the entire time, it was a much needed, rare weekend away for Scott and I. The five-hour car ride alone would be a precious gift of devoted time together.

The conference was held at the Hilton in the Back Bay of Boston. When we walked in and saw hundreds of other parents occupying the space of the expansive banquet room, I wanted to cry tears of relief and joy. I shuddered at the sudden surge of emotion which made the hair on my arms stand up out of all the tiny goosebumps covering my skin. My eyes scanned the room slowly, taking it all in. The floor had a burgundy red carpet with a beige paisley-like design. Gold-rimmed chairs with red velvet upholstery filled many aisles from the stage to the back of the room where we entered. The message was loud and clear: You are not alone.

The three-day conference had already kicked off, and I could feel the common cause in the room buzzing like an electric current that ran through all of us. We were all connected by our intrigue with autism and our dedication to finding a healing path for our children, even if it was the road less traveled. I glanced at the man sitting next to me who looked to be the same age as me. His attention was 100 percent on the speaker as if his life depended on what that doctor was saying. Curious, I imagined if he, too, had a child with autism, and if his child was as sick as Kelly—if he screams in fits of anger or bangs his head on the floor? Does his kid sleep? What does he eat? Does it make him uncontrollably sick?

Within minutes, like the man next to me, my attention and Scott's attention was glued to the podium and whoever was presenting. We listened as Karyn Seroussi shared the story of her son's gut issues. I couldn't believe we were learning about the questions that had been tormenting my mind for so many months. Karyn referenced her book, *Unraveling the Mystery of Autism and Pervasive Developmental Disorder: A Mother's Story of Research & Recovery*, in which she discusses how many autistic children have abnormal gut permeability, forcing them to act out from the pain and discomfort. I wondered what the other people in the room were thinking. Were they—like me—feeling relieved, validated, and more hopeful for solutions?

Karyn went on to explain that antibiotics kill off naturally existing healthy flora in the intestines, which then leads to overgrowth of unhealthy bacteria and yeast. She discussed the theory that the protein in milk and dairy has an opiate effect on the brain, making it addictive. My mind raced. I needed to know more. I felt like we were finding missing pieces to Kelly's puzzle, the links to help us finally understand her symptoms, thoughts, and behaviors.

Lisa Lewis, author of *Special Diets for Special Kids*, enlightened the crowd with her blanket recommendation of a gluten-free, casein-free (GFCF) diet that also restricted sugar. Lisa referred to the immune system dysfunction component of autism, which leads to food intolerances, including the inability to break down casein and gluten as well as phenolic foods like bananas, tomatoes, soy, corn, and apples.

One DAN doctor told the story of how a patient of his, a young boy, snuck into his mom's bathroom and drank an entire bottle of her liquid foundation makeup. His cravings for gluten were so strong that the boy was looking for it anywhere and everywhere. I felt lucky that Kelly's cravings weren't that intense. I prayed they never got to that point. I was reminded that no matter how bad you think you have it, there's always someone who has it worse than you.

Finally, it was time for Dr. Baker's presentation.

I leaned over and whispered to Scott: "This is the guy that Lisa wants us to meet. He's the doctor that helped Connor. I'm hoping he will also help Kelly." Dr. Baker's PowerPoint included a slide with a photograph of Connor, Lisa's son. He shared the approach he was taking with Connor and other patients, explaining their progress in detail. His focus was on healing the gut.

While in school, I never considered myself to have a science brain. It didn't click for me and I wasn't drawn to it, so I avoided those classes. But sitting in the conference room that day, something in me was turned on. I was attracted to the process of taking a guess, making a hypothesis, testing it, collecting the results, and presenting the evidence as truth. That's how new, revolutionary practices were started. That's how these doctors were paving cutting-edge paths to healthier lifestyles for many kids, to hope for many parents. Science was the only way out. Particularly, I was seeing how food played a principle role. Every speaker had something to say about the relationship between autism and diet. Some stories were more dramatic than others, but transformation was still present in most cases.

They were spinning a web across all the ideas I'd never thought to connect—diet choices, eating schedules, digestion, behavior, mood swings, sleep, pain, and chronic sickness. I began to see the bigger picture, the biology and biochemistry behind all of it. For the first time, I started to rethink the euphemism that we are what we eat, or don't eat. I wrote it down, trying to cement the belief in my brain.

In Kelly's case, knowledge of science was power, and after so many months living in fear and lack of control, I wanted as much of that power over our lifestyle as I could get. My mind was a sponge, and I wrote fervently in each session, ignoring my tired hand. I put value in every word. Scott and I stuck together as if we were part of the group, but separate. We introduced ourselves to a few parents, but mostly kept to ourselves. Newbies, we were still digesting it all.

After two days and a dozen or so speakers, it was time to go home. Tilling the tough memories of Kelly's past year, I had a newfound respect and appreciation for the DAN doctors and their research. They were starting to look like heroes in my mind. As we stood up to leave, I glanced around the room at the sea of parents—those I'd met and those I wanted to know but hadn't met yet—and it was so clear that all of our kids needed a hero. This was just the beginning.

On the trip home, Scott and I talked about all the nuggets we would take home from the conference. The same speakers stuck with both of us—they were the ones that spoke closely to the factors and experiences that we'd been facing with Kelly. While Scott drove, I rattled off thoughts, reviewed my notes, and processed what we'd learned. Within the bubble of our car windows, fresh with new knowledge and boosted by the common journey of so many parents, I shared that I was convinced there was an organic component to autism. What had been bothering me for months finally bubbled up to the surface. I told Scott I thought the root of Kelly's problem was being overlooked by standard medical practice. He agreed and was open, ready to try the DAN approach.

Since we'd heard so many speakers talk about the important link between diet and behavior, I thought I should start by keeping a journal. As soon as I got home, I immediately did two things: I called Dr. Baker's office to get on the waiting list, and I started a journal to track Kelly's diet and corresponding behaviors.

It would be at least six months before Dr. Baker had an opening. Though I was disappointed, I expected that much. So I had a plan for collecting data in the meantime. I'd continue documenting. I began writing down every item of food that Kelly ate and every behavior that seemed abnormal—every incident of obstinate yelling, rage, complaint of pain, nausea, bowel movement, or outrageous reaction. Sometimes I couldn't write fast enough because the behaviors happened as often as twenty times in an hour.

The documentation of events turned our day into one long but welcome science experiment and added an element of intrigue. While it was still hard to handle and witness, the journaling managed to remove some of the emotional attachment to every punch or revolt. Seeing it in writing clarified that I wasn't exaggerating or imagining her behaviors to be worse or better than they were. As I wrote, it was validation for me to keep digging, keep examining, keep fighting.

7

eating to not be sick

"Always love. No matter how many times you get hurt,
keep loving because love is good and love always brings
out the best in people."

A few weeks after the DAN conference, I decided I couldn't wait six months and called Dr. Baker's assistant to get a recommendation of someone that worked with him. She suggested we see a nurse practitioner, Marilyn, who consulted with Dr. Baker and could get us started with some testing and dietary guidance.

Since Marilyn's office was two and a half hours away from our house, my mom agreed to come with me to entertain Kelly and help navigate the trip. She was great with Kelly—engaging her in backseat story time and eventually settling her into the ride with laughter and song, just like she'd done before.

Marilyn was a one-woman show, the complete opposite of Dr. Johnson's office which buzzed with nurses, doctors, and a constant flow of patients. Marilyn's suite was in a wooded office park and looked more like a condominium or apartment than a medical office. Inside the entrance was an area for the kids to play with some toys, and off to the left was a small room with one exam table, a scale, and a chair. The walls were covered in a sun-stained, flowered wallpaper—a pattern that was popular decades ago. It was peeling around the edges along the woodwork that was painted dark green. My mom played with Kelly over in the toy corner while I filled out the necessary paperwork and reviewed Kelly's medical history with Marilyn.

Marilyn wanted to know everything about Kelly's current diet, what she ate on a daily basis, and any medications or treatments we'd tried so far. I referred to my journal entries.

"What about giving Kelly chicken or turkey for a snack instead of cookies?" Marilyn recommended. At first, I thought that'd be an impossible feat. *How the heck will I get Kelly to accept chicken as a snack when she's used to eating Oreos and Goldfish?* The last thing I could endure would be more tantrums or violent outbursts, especially ones that I triggered.

"Okay, maybe," I responded, unconvinced that this would fly with Kelly. Marilyn went on to explain why she suggested that. Protein would help stabilize Kelly's blood sugar and thus regulate her moods.

Like flipping on a light switch, suddenly, it hit me. The fun, colorfully wrapped, cool-shaped stuff was all a gimmick to coax kids to convince their parents to buy junk food. Or rather, for parents like me, to feel like they were doing something nice or rewarding for their kids and to distract or encourage compliance. Like when Natalie was a toddler and I pushed her in the Baby Jogger while I ran, her little hands feeding her mouth Goldfish crackers the entire way.

I liked that Marilyn was putting healthy food in its proper place as a priority in Kelly's daily routine. I told myself I could shift my thinking.

I confessed to Marilyn how much Kelly loved orange juice. She drank several glasses a day. Her orange juice was like a blankie— the thing children can't sleep without and snuggle with while sucking their thumb. Kelly clung to her sippy cup of orange juice for comfort. After drinking a few loud gulps, she'd sigh, lick her lips, and then smile a satisfied grin.

"Forget the juice," Marilyn blurted out in a matter-of-fact tone. "It's full of empty calories and the sugar in it is feeding the yeast, or bad guys, in her gut." I'd heard about this at the DAN conference. I still didn't completely understand this concept of "bad guys" in the gut, but believed it to be true.

Nodding my head enthusiastically, I listened to Marilyn's diet suggestions and new, healthy regimen. Whenever negativity, guilt, and doubt crept into my mind, I dismissed them. I was driven to keep an open mind. I'd deal with any backlash later.

After about thirty minutes of a thorough intake on Kelly's medical history, Marilyn asked Kelly if she could take a look at her.

"Sure," Kelly agreed.

Marilyn got her to sit on the exam table and did a brief physical, including checking Kelly's fingernails and toenails for fungus. Marilyn recommended bloodwork to check Kelly's liver enzymes along with other markers, plus a test for delayed food allergies or intolerances.

"This is a different type of allergy testing," she explained. "It's a blood test that will detect an antibody response, specifically IgG antibody response, to food sensitivities or delayed food reactions," she elaborated. "The reaction causes a wide spectrum of symptoms depending on the individual, which show up hours, sometimes days, after eating the food, making them difficult to detect without this type of testing." I'd never heard of this before, but it made sense.

This was the first extensive and helpful dialogue I'd had with anyone about diet and its connection to Kelly's symptoms and behaviors. Finally, we had a concrete plan. Marilyn handed me a list that included instructions on food testing, stool samples to be shipped to a lab, scripts for specific bloodwork, supplements to start after the testing, and dietary advice.

"So, Kelly will need to have a blood test?" I confirmed. Instead of the typical apprehension I'd felt around Kelly's medical tests, I was eager and willing to try whatever Marilyn prescribed.

"Yes, and I'll give you a numbing cream to apply one hour

before. Kelly won't feel a thing," Marilyn answered, reassuring me.

During the drive home, when I shared my enthusiasm about Marilyn, my mom muttered a few of her "what ifs," laden with undertones of disbelief. I tried convincing myself that she just wanted to protect Kelly and me, but in my mind, it was obvious she didn't understand how I could trust Marilyn instead of a more professional, well-known doctor.

I wanted to remind her that we already went to a recommended specialist, the best in the area. I wanted to remind her of my many months of frustration without a diagnosis, or a plan, or any support from a doctor or his staff. I wanted to remind her that I knew what was best for my daughter, that I'd put in the hard work to figure it out, and that this was our new path.

Instead, I kept all the disappointment inside, swirling around in my head. Having overcome my own initial hesitation, I was already committed to trying absolutely everything if it could potentially be the magic bullet that would help Kelly get better. I decided not to pay attention to the doubt and criticism. I simply didn't have space for it.

By this time, it was obvious Kelly needed help beyond what conventional medicine had to offer. In my mind, we had no choice. I was motivated by how physically sick Kelly looked. She had large, dark, puffy circles under her eyes and her cheeks had a greyish hue. Her belly stuck out in a hard, distended ball, while her arms and legs were bony thin. Instead of being white, the enamel on her baby teeth looked a dull yellowish grey, and her smile was not accompanied by sparkling eyes. Instead, her blue eyes were distant and lost. It was impossible to ignore the things that were staring right at me, begging my attention.

While I was starting to understand the role of food and was committed to giving those changes a try, I saw it more as a solution to Kelly's tummy troubles. Another part of me questioned if we shouldn't just give Kelly medication to calm her irritability, mood swings, inability to focus, and hyperactivity. I wasn't convinced that food could change all that.

The neuropsychologist who'd done IQ and other testing on Kelly described Kelly by saying, "She is easily distracted and has extremely weak mental control. ADD and ADHD typically go along with PDD and autism." He recommended medication for Kelly— Buspar and Concerta. I began to wonder if maybe medication was a necessary evil, if maybe it was the only way to get some relief.

Not sure what to do, I asked one of my friends who had a son with autism. She suggested Celexa. They'd tried Concerta and Risperdal without much luck.

"Medication can really help with self-esteem, or when anxiety gets too high that it is interfering with decisions," was her endorsement. I began to feel as if medication was an inevitable solution and that I was doing a disservice to Kelly by not medicating her.

Desperate for some sort of reprieve, I decided to consider medication and made an appointment with Dr. Altman, the psychiatrist who diagnosed Kelly with autism. Just sitting with someone who wouldn't judge me, who understood where I was coming from, and being able to release all the frustration that my body had been bottling up was a relief. Leaning back into the comfortable leather chair in her office, I felt like twenty pounds had been lifted off my shoulders.

The previous spring, Dr. Altman went to the DAN conference with my friend and autism mentor, Mary Barbera. So I knew she would understand the more holistic approach I wanted to take with Kelly, including all the dietary changes we were implementing.

"Here's a prescription for Prozac, but try the DAN approach first," was her advice. I felt better just knowing I had a prescription as an option.

When I got home, I chose to put the little white square piece of paper in Kelly's medical file. Despite my exhaustion, the stress, and my inability to sleep or relax, I resigned to the fact that I just couldn't give Kelly a drug for her behaviors, not yet. Even though it was a tempting magic pill, I really didn't want to go down that path. It just didn't feel right. It felt like that'd be cheating, taking the easy way out. The same intuition that nudged me to explore holistic healing, the DAN approach, was begging me to keep the faith and not give in to medication no matter how bad it got.

Scott and I were on the same page. I drew strength and confidence from his trust and unwavering love. We each had our own roles, a sort of unspoken agreement. He worked every day, all day, making sure we had the money to pay our bills and finance Kelly's treatment plan. I managed all of Kelly's therapies, doctor appointments, diet, and supplements. He trusted me in the driver's seat, trusted me to take the lead with Kelly.

Two months after seeing Marilyn, I had a phone consult with her to review Kelly's test results. Eighty-eight different foods were tested, and Kelly tested positive to twenty-five of them. Some of the foods she needed to avoid included citrus (in all its forms—that's right, no more orange juice), bananas, eggs, dairy, kidney beans, corn, soy, green beans, canola oil, and peanuts. Kelly's bloodwork also revealed that she had celiac disease, so gluten was out, too. Marilyn recommended protein-based foods at every meal and offered alternatives while we spoke for almost an hour.

Having grown up on them, Kelly loved pretzels. The only pretzels that were gluten-free were made with corn; so, no more pretzels either. For all the other things like cookies, ice cream, bread, and waffles, I found alternatives. I decided that in order to keep myself sane and committed to the plan, instead of thinking of all the foods she couldn't eat, I would focus on what Kelly *could* eat.

Her meals consisted of meat, vegetables, and gluten-free grains like white rice, brown rice noodles, and potatoes. Snacks were Nature's Path Crispy Rice Bars, potato chips, and spicy brown rice crackers, which Kelly would just lick the seasoning off of, leaving the cracker behind. Kelly drank rice milk and ate Rice Dream ice cream and popsicles. Marilyn recommended brown rice protein powder to make a protein shake. Since Kelly couldn't have eggs or dairy, I used palm oil shortening and applesauce for baking. One of her big treats was going to McDonald's. Kelly got a plain burger, no bun, with fries.

In the beginning, I felt like I was hurting Kelly in some way by not allowing her to have her favorite foods. Every time she whined or begged for her old favorites—the Oreos, orange juice, pizza, pretzels, or ice cream—doubt clouded my decision-making. Denying her those pleasures made me feel like the antihero. I questioned if all the effort put into this new regimen would really make a difference. I feared that Kelly would become even more distant if I was too controlling with food. That was probably why I didn't demand that Natalie eat what Kelly was eating. Yet, the uncertainty that crept into my thoughts was really about my own fear and guilt.

Besides Lisa, no one else in our community was following a diet like this or understood why I was doing it. All the kids in school or friends from the neighborhood were snacking on Goldfish, pretzels, and Oreo cookies, including Natalie. I still bought Oreos, ice cream, pizza, and gluten-full bread for Natalie and Scott. Natalie had already been subjected to enough inconvenience and embarrassment from Kelly's behaviors and therapies that I didn't want to subject her to being gluten-free too.

One morning, a few weeks after eliminating Kelly's food triggers, her cute little button nose and sweet rosy lips looked up at me, pleading for a glass of orange juice. I stared at her beautiful blonde hair and blue eyes and decided that one glass couldn't hurt. The tantrums began almost immediately after she drank the juice. Something came over her, like she was possessed by a demon that needed to be exorcised. Her body trembled with energy as her hands rapidly flapped in an inimitable stim—a self-stimulatory behavior that's a common symptom of autism. Then she got really angry, started throwing things, and couldn't hear or see what was happening around her. Kelly was irrational and out of control, all triggered by a glass of orange juice.

It was in that moment that it became vividly clear to me that what Kelly ate—or, in this case, drank—was directly connected to her behaviors and mood. I realized with complete conviction that this was not a scam. It was real science. I saw, for the first time in my life, that food can be harmful, detrimental even, to our health and well-being. Like an earthquake caused by a sudden break along the fault of the earth's plates, this was a massive shift in how I viewed eating, and it rocked me to the core.

I started reading labels fanatically, calling companies to find out about ingredients, and, out of default, became the food police, monitoring everything that went in Kelly's mouth. In fact, it obsessed me. Even the tiniest crumbs of gluten on the counter began to freak me out and for a good reason.

Finally, we were seeing some positive results. Over the next few weeks, Kelly was making a turn for the better. She was sleeping more soundly and her eyes were less puffy. The dark-grey circles and colorless palette turned to delicate, porcelain-beige skin like her big sister's.

"Why is Kelly allergic to milk?" Natalie asked me one morning at the breakfast table.

Before I could answer, Kelly started crying and yelling: "I don't have lergic in my body!"

Later, when it was just Natalie and I in the kitchen, I told her, "Kelly's stomach can't digest milk and the other foods she's sensitive to. I don't really know why, but I think it's kind of like her body thinks those foods are the bad guys."

Kelly was six years old and Natalie was eight. In second grade, Natalie had become an avid reader, devouring books at home and those her class read in school. *Misty of Chincoteague* and *Mr. Popper's Penguins* were two of her favorites. Natalie's pace in acquiring new skills and learning was much faster than her sister's and many of her friends'. Whether it was her nature or she was forced to because of the disruption at home, Natalie was maturing at a rapid rate.

I tried, maybe in vain, to preserve pieces of Natalie's normal world, those pieces unaffected by all the changes going on in Kelly's and mine. Natalie had a new best friend from her class at school. Several times a week, she'd go over to her friend's house to play after school, which was a blessing.

On Wednesday afternoons, while Kelly was at speech therapy, Natalie and I would sit in the hospital cafeteria and eat M&M's from the vending machine. Other times, we'd get back in the car and drive down the street to Dairy Queen for ice cream. Reese's Peanut Butter Cup Blizzards were my favorite and Natalie's was a dish of vanilla soft serve with rainbow sprinkles. I cherished the few hours we had alone every week, even if it was at the hospital.

Natalie was often the brunt of Kelly's anger. Even though I believed Kelly didn't really mean it, I worried about the effect this would have on Natalie. I knew Kelly loved her big sister, but whenever Natalie would talk to me, it prompted some kind of interruption and negative reaction from Kelly. Then, Kelly would blame Natalie for things like breaking her necklace or stealing her belts.

"Kelly, I didn't take your belt." Natalie tried helping by explaining things or setting Kelly straight, even in the midst of repeated false accusations. Often it was futile. No matter what Natalie said, Kelly's protests only grew louder, as if she never heard Natalie. When I watched Natalie's calm, matter-of-fact response to Kelly's tantrums, I couldn't believe how lucky I was to have an eight-year-old whose first instinct was to help by teaching or correcting the situation. Every now and then, Natalie would snap, but for the most part, she tried to remove herself from the scene.

At the time, Kelly's therapy was following a regular schedule. She had speech therapy three times a week, occupational therapy three times a week, and wraparound therapists either in our home or at school for a total of twenty-eight hours a week. Everyone had their specific role. Judy, the occupational therapist, was there to help Kelly break out of rigidity, teach her hand-eye coordination, and dull her sensory overload. In speech therapy, the therapist did exercises with Kelly to decrease frustration through improved comprehension, processing, and vocabulary. Using applied behavior analysis (ABA) techniques, wraparound targeted specific behaviors by teaching coping and cognitive skills like learning the calendar, time, and sequencing of events. The overall goals were to reduce the tantrums, irrational outbursts, grabbing, impulsive hitting, and lashing out.

I shared my intentions to change Kelly's diet and my optimism that it would impact her behaviors with Kelly's behavior specialist, Robin, who was particularly supportive. She had observed Kelly crying, doubled over in pain on the floor in the middle of therapy sessions. One day, when talking with Robin alone, I openly vented my frustration over Kelly's erratic behaviors and food challenges. Robin's intent gaze, expressive hazel-green eyes, and relaxed smile put me at ease. She leaned in toward me while explaining Kelly in the best possible way, one that showed both her empathy and expertise in the field of autism.

"The trouble is she's got such an adorable face," Robin confessed with a slight laugh. It was true. Kelly's sweet face made me melt. Like me, Robin believed in Kelly's underlying happy spirit. That was what drove our mutual intention with therapy—to uncover that positive side of Kelly. Putting aside emotion, Robin's role was to reinforce, over and over again, that the therapy would help Kelly, even if it was hard work.

As a behavior specialist, Robin directed Kelly's wraparound services and wrote the goals for Kelly's treatment plan. She then directed activities for the therapeutic support staff (TSS) that worked with Kelly. Robin was a trained counselor with her master's. Where we were still learning, she fully comprehended what made Kelly tick. With a strong understanding of autism, Robin was sensitive and alert to Kelly's needs and also acknowledged her strengths by using them as a way to motivate Kelly. I liked Robin's style. She appealed to the creative side of Kelly and was also cognizant of Natalie and Scott and how the family unit worked.

With ABA, one of the goals was to extinguish unwanted behaviors using a principle called "extinction." Extinction aimed to remove the reinforcement of a behavior. Robin taught me that by responding to Kelly's outbursts, we'd been reinforcing, or strengthening, them.

"Any and all attention given to a behavior will increase the occurrence of it. That's behavior 101." Robin was training me too. It made so much sense. I just never thought of it before. We needed to be black and white. There could be no grey with Kelly.

"Ignore Kelly whenever she screams or hits," Robin instructed me. "Give attention to Natalie, remove it from Kelly."

It was my job to translate these strategies to Scott so we could all be on the same page. Consistency was key. This was the only way it would work. While it sounded so simple, Scott, Natalie, and I found it nearly impossible to follow through. We learned the hard way that the typical response to the initial extinction trials often resulted in increased, intensified negative behavior. This was called an "extinction burst," Robin told us. Each time we tried to ignore Kelly, her frustration would escalate. This made it even harder to have faith in the plan. But we had no choice.

The way I saw it, diet and supplements would tackle whatever had a hold on Kelly from the inside, and therapy would work on it from the outside.

After following Marilyn's instructions for almost a year, in early December of 2002, Kelly had her initial appointment with Dr. Baker at his office in Connecticut. Based on the testing that Marilyn did, which showed Kelly had almost zero good bacteria in her gut, Dr. Baker theorized that Kelly had dysbiosis, a microbial imbalance.

In other words, Kelly had either a severe deficiency of healthy good bacteria, or an overgrowth of harmful bacteria in her digestive tract. He theorized that this could have been from multiple rounds of antibiotics she took as a toddler for ear and sinus infections. The visual symptom of dysbiosis was her distended stomach that resembled a hard, round protruding belly—just like a beer belly on a man that drank often. It was so strange to see this on my blonde, blue-eyed little girl.

Dr. Baker wanted Kelly to try a protocol he termed an "antifungal parade." His intention with using antifungals was to eliminate the overgrowth of yeast or other harmful bacteria in her gut. Through process of elimination, we'd find which antifungal worked best for Kelly.

"It's different for each child. What works for one doesn't always work for another," Dr. Baker explained.

This systematic plan took about a year, and sure enough, we tried five or six different prescriptions before finding the winner. For Kelly, Lamisil was the one that regularly gave the best results. When she took Lamisil, she calmed down, was less irritable, became more focused, and consistently slept through the night.

No matter what we said or approach we presented, we couldn't convince Kelly to swallow pills. So, I crushed the Lamisil tablet and put it in applesauce along with her supplements—a multivitamin, calcium, and magnesium. As the spoon entered her mouth, Kelly gagged on the mountain of applesauce stuffed with white, chalky powder. Some days, she ran away at the sight of it. To help with compliance, we started a sticker reward program just to get her to take the medicine every day. After getting fifteen stickers, she could get a new Barbie doll.

One day, a few weeks after starting Lamisil, we were at the hospital for Kelly's speech therapy appointment. Miss Pamela, Kelly's speech therapist, asked me if Kelly was on medication, something we'd never discussed before. I worried that she was going to reject our unconventional approach.

"Yes," I said, hesitating to give specifics. "She's on an antifungal right now that seems to be working quite well."

"I have known Kelly for almost three years, and this is the only time I've ever seen her like this," Miss Pamela reported. Her approach was diligent and professional, but business-like and aligned with Robin's strategies. Miss Pamela extinguished negative behaviors by completely removing her attention from the child. When Kelly grabbed Miss Pamela's skirt to feel the fabric and then told her she looked pretty, Miss Pamela just pushed Kelly's hand away without saying a word about it.

"Like what?" I asked, worried.

"She's less moody and more focused, talkative, and engaged in the tasks. And her scores show noticeable improvement," Miss Pamela continued in a bubbly voice, her gracious and happy expression showing that she was pleased.

As soon as Kelly went off the Lamisil or we changed the dose even the slightest bit, she immediately regressed to eloping from tasks, yelling, flapping her hands, making baby talk, and touching everything excessively for sensory input. Smells bothered her, and she refused to eat certain textures of food. Worst of all, she wouldn't sleep all night.

Based on Kelly's response to the antifungal, I began to understand that her gut was at the center of her issues, that it was connected to her brain, not a planet all its own. The way I saw it, the food Kelly had been eating acted like poison to her belly and brain.

Allowing her to eat whatever she wanted just because I sympathized with her wasn't a good strategy. Giving up because a little extra planning or cooking was too much work wasn't an option either. I knew that I needed to commit to this way of life, to her eating what her body and brain needed. In doing so, I'd be honoring Kelly, and myself as her mother. Once I saw that clearly and made the decision to stick to it, there was no turning back.

The next step was that I needed to teach Kelly how and what to eat to feel good. My goal was for her to listen to her body and understand how food affected her. Her choices would be about eating to not be sick. I didn't want her to think I was just trying to control her or fix her. I wanted her to be the happy, loving spirit she was meant to be. I was doing all of it because I believed in her. I believed in us.

8

connecting the dots

*"Every living thing has a spirit whether they're aware of it or
not, and everyone connects in some kind of way."*

She can't be the only one. I thought about Kelly's food sensitivities
and her complicated, diverse reactions. One morning while I was
reflecting on her new diet, it dawned on me like it'd never occurred
to me before. And it hadn't. Perhaps, for her, it was more dramatic,
but either way, I began connecting the dots between Kelly's intolerances and my own relationship with food.

I was five years old.

"Mom!" I cried out in pain, tears dribbling down my cheeks as
I sat on the toilet. Elbows resting on my knees, with my chin in
the palms of my hands, the minutes passed while I stared down at
the white and beige squares on the shiny linoleum bathroom floor.
The straining hurt my small body. I was constipated and cramp-
ing which went along with my chronic bellyaches and headaches.
Whenever I got stuck on the potty, I always called out to Mom.

"Oh, honey." My mom sighed when she found me stuck on the
toilet again. It happened often, maybe once a week.

"Here, drink this," she'd say, handing me a glass of orange juice
for the constipation.

The summer after I finished first grade, my grandparents
planned a vacation at a dude ranch in Montana for our family plus

all six of my mom's brothers and sisters. As the only grandkids, three of my four sisters and I also got to go along. Prior to the trip, it was required that we take horseback riding lessons. Six years old, I absolutely loved sitting up high on the horse's back, feeling the unconstrained exhilaration of letting such a graceful animal take me for a ride. It was like the horse and I became one. The faster the horse ran, the greater the natural high I felt. I couldn't wait to get to the ranch knowing I'd be riding every day.

On the morning of our flight to Montana, that familiar and unpleasant feeling was back in my stomach and there was a dull ache across my forehead. I couldn't find my mom so I decided to break the bad news to my dad who had no patience or empathy for sickness.

"I have a headache and . . . ," I began, hesitating to continue. "My belly hurts." I whimpered, sniffling and staring at the ground to avoid Dad's inevitably patronizing glare. I clutched my belly with my arms while my eyes glazed over from the tears I tried holding back. Not only did I feel sick, but I didn't want to be left behind like my youngest sister who, at age two, was too young to go on the trip.

My dad just looked at me with his piercing glacial-blue eyes and rebutted, "You're not sick!"

Of course, it was terribly inconvenient timing on my part, but I couldn't help it.

"Here, take these," he said, giving me two pink chewable baby aspirin before we got in the car to drive to the airport.

After I grabbed the blue barf bag out of the back pocket of the airplane seat and threw up, I wanted to correct my dad and announce, "See, I told you I was sick!" But I resisted the temptation for fear of a public scolding and more embarrassment. Instead, I hunched over in my seat, covering my mouth with my hands. My belly felt slightly better, emptied from whatever was ailing me. Mom handed me some tissues, then gently rubbed my shoulder with her hand before returning to her seat next to my younger sister.

Growing up, I would often wake up feeling queasy. If I ate cereal, it would make my stomach even more nauseous, and I'd be hungry again soon after eating it. As badly as I wanted to munch on a bowl of brightly colored, fruity Trix cereal covered in milk, or to pick the red cherry-flavored balls out of the Captain Crunch cereal box, all the fun-looking sugary cereals just didn't agree with me.

When I was around ten years old, one morning, instead of eating cereal, I asked my mom if she would make me a hamburger for breakfast. Hamburgers tasted good, and I liked how I felt more energetic and focused after eating one. Mom didn't complain about my unusual and more labor-intensive breakfast request. I think she could sense that I really just wanted to feel alert and calm inside after eating.

Most days, when I'd walk in the kitchen for breakfast, my mom would look at me and in a clumsy attempt to comfort me would say, "Honey, you look so tired." Since I hardly wanted to be reminded of the fact that I had perpetual puffy dark circles under my eyes, I ignored her. Even though my mom empathized with me, I didn't want to be a complainer. I began keeping my aches and pains to myself, internalizing any physical or emotional discomfort. Instead of saying I had a stomachache, I'd retreat to my room and lie in bed, clutching my pillow while trying to read or listen to music. Our petite, short-haired cat, Tiffany, and I shared long conversations about imaginary magical places while I lay in bed. When I felt especially sick, I'd listen to her purr while stroking her silky white fur to relax—an undeclared natural, homemade therapy.

I felt like it was my fault that I looked tired, my fault that I kept getting strep throat, and that my stomachaches were interpreted as merely figments of my imagination. I guess my symptoms were too mysterious to investigate. No one ever considered that I might have allergies, seasonal or food-related. I went through adolescence, my teens, and early twenties before getting it checked out.

Years later, these childhood bouts were a distant memory. Then, one day, while I was working at Dun & Bradstreet in Boston, the job I'd started right after graduating from college, I went to the ladies' room. The peach-colored sinks had fancy brass fixtures and the floor was shiny white marble tile. While in the stall, after wiping, I noticed the toilet paper was stained red. Since I didn't have my period, I began to panic. Then, when I stood up to throw the toilet paper in the toilet, I saw the water in toilet bowl was also red from blood.

In disbelief, I flushed to make the evidence disappear and quickly pulled my pantyhose up then smoothed the fabric of my skirt, rubbing my hands over my thighs several times. While washing my hands, I stared at my reflection in the gold-framed mirror. Glossy, mocha-colored lipstick rolled over my lips in a cleansing motion. *It's probably nothing*, I reassured myself.

These episodes happened maybe five or six more times over several months before I made an appointment with an internist. It was the fall of 1989. After an hour of questions about my medical history and a thorough physical exam, he recommended a procedure called a sigmoidoscopy.

"It looks like you have ulcers that are causing the bleeding," he told me after the camera finished exploring my rectum and colon. At the time, there was no treatment recommendation or medication, so I never did anything about it.

Then, a few months later, while sitting at my desk at work, another mysterious symptom appeared. As I ran my fingers through my hair, I noticed scabs on my scalp. I'd never felt them before and wondered where they came from. The crusty spots would get itchy, especially if I exercised or whenever I sweat. The more I scratched, the more they itched, just like poison ivy. After itching the spots, my finger was tacky and covered with puss. I tried a special shampoo and a topical ointment for itchy scalp, but nothing helped.

After months of having the annoying scabs on my scalp, out

of the blue, as I reached back to pull up my hair, I noticed I had swollen lumps behind my ears on my neck. The bumps were tender and hurt when I ran my fingers over them. Though they were similar in shape and size, they were different than the swollen glands I'd get with a sore throat—those weren't painfully tender like the ones on the back of my neck. I began to worry that maybe the scabs were an infection and were causing the swollen painful lumps that I guessed were my lymph nodes.

Concerned, I made an appointment with a dermatologist in Boston. I'd never met her before. As I told her my story, her long blonde hair tipped to one side while she stared at me, her hands tucked in the pockets of her white lab coat.

Her nose wrinkled while she interrogated me in a condescending tone: "Are you sure they just appeared?"

"Yes," I replied, clenching my teeth together.

I crossed my arms over my chest in embarrassment, befuddled by the way her eyes scanned me like I'd done something wrong to create the itchy scabs. Then came the diagnosis. Folliculitis.

"You need to stop picking at your head or your hair will never grow back," she threatened.

The thought of balding scared me, especially if my scalp was covered with scabs. Yet, I hardly believed I was to blame for their sudden appearance. The dermatologist treated it as a bacterial infection and prescribed antibiotics.

When the scabs resurfaced a few months later, after I'd finished the antibiotic, I decided to get a second opinion and went to my mom's dermatologist in Pennsylvania.

"The problem is you need to stop exercising. Sweating is causing these symptoms," he concluded, prescribing a topical steroid cream.

I wasn't going to stop exercising. That was a ridiculous recommendation. I knew exercise wasn't my problem. It was merely exacerbating my symptoms. My problem was whatever was causing my skin to be inflamed, itchy, and purulent. *Why aren't they trying to figure that out?* Not knowing what else to do, I relied on the prescription cream for years. Later on, I learned that folliculitis is usually caused by an internal fungal infection.

Around the same time that Kelly was diagnosed with autism and was having all her tummy troubles, another symptom manifested in my body. I developed chronic neck pain. My head felt like a bowling ball, heavy and wobbly, on top of my long, skinny neck. It was difficult to turn my head to either side as I was backing up my car in a parking lot or switching lanes while driving. Every time I had to bend over to pick up toys off the floor, I winced and grunted from the pain that throbbed in my neck as I moved.

For months on end, simply standing put a strain on my neck as evidenced by a dull, deep ache. At night, I could sleep for about four hours before I'd wake up, unable to get comfortable. Pillows propped my head up on either side, and under my knees were more pillows to help ease the pain. My own pain and Kelly's night terrors were my two reliable companions that prevented me from sleeping.

Ten years earlier, when we got married, Scott and I declared to each other that we would never have our own sides of the bed. Newlyweds, we slept like a pretzel with our legs tangled around each other while my arm cuddled his waist or his mine. Now, the mountain of pillows I'd piled around me felt like a wall between the two of us. My side was the left side of the bed, with Scott on my right, because I could only comfortably sleep on my back or on my right side. If there was even a slim chance of us snuggling, he needed to be on my right—that was the rule.

I was thirty-four years old, but with the way I slept and spent my day in discomfort, it seemed like I was a seventy-year-old woman, complaining all day of the aches and pains of aging.

Feeling debilitated, exhausted, and longing for some kind of pain relief, I went to see an orthopedic doctor. A bone scan revealed Raynaud's syndrome and arthritis in my neck. The doctor also reconfirmed the thoracic outlet syndrome I'd been diagnosed with at age eighteen as a result of my scoliosis.

"For pain, the best thing is to take Advil 800 mg three times a day," he instructed. He also prescribed physical therapy.

After about six months of physical therapy and Advil around the clock, my pain hadn't improved much. A pain management doctor was the next step. When that doctor told me, "antidepressants are extremely effective in treating chronic pain," I thought he was trying to tell me I was merely imagining my physical suffering. I didn't want to take mind-altering drugs, especially since I hadn't been diagnosed with depression or any other mental health issue. So I never filled the prescription. Although I still went about my daily activities without having to ask for help, my body and mind were drained by the constant pain.

The orthopedist sent me to a specialist, a surgeon who could handle the complicating factors of my symptoms. When the specialist said, "You need to decide if you want to have surgery," I was relieved at the possibility of a solution to take my pain away. But he advised that surgery could leave me with scar tissue that may cause as much or more pain than I already had at the time. That made me decide against surgery, and I resigned myself to a new strategy—trying to trick myself into thinking my pain wasn't as bad as I thought.

The exhaustion from physical pain and lack of sleep left me feeling despondent and discouraged with my own personal routine, or absence of one. Clogged from all the stress, I searched for ways to indulge myself—secret boosts of artificial energy and mindless escape in sugar and sweets. Almost every day, I'd make a batch of homemade chocolate chip cookies. Butter, flour, sugar, and chocolate—what a dreamy concoction of deliciousness. I ate four or five fresh-baked cookies every afternoon while Kelly was working in the basement with her therapists.

Whenever I heard Kelly yell in protest to challenging tasks she dreaded, I'd have one more cookie, and then another. At the end of the session, when the therapist walked up into the kitchen from the basement, I'd hand her a paper plate piled with warm cookies and covered with tinfoil. Although I worried the entire time Kelly was alone with the therapists, I was also incredibly grateful that they were willing to work with her. The break was a gift, even if all I managed to do was bake cookies and tinker around the house washing fingerprint marks off the walls, cleaning bathrooms, or dusting baseboards.

Most days, Scott would leave before eight in the morning and come home at seven o'clock at night. By the time he walked in the door, the pots were boiling. I'd be slumped over the stove, cooking dinner, while also trying to keep Kelly entertained at the table and away from Natalie so Kelly wouldn't yell at or hit her. Scott walked into a house of palpable tension. My face was so tightly twisted from pain and stress that I couldn't unravel it no matter how hard I tried. One day, he came over to the stove and put his hands on my shoulders.

"Just be happy," he said calmly, lovingly.

That day in particular, he hadn't checked in with me once. I was overwhelmed, uncomfortable, and annoyed. Just like my dad, Scott didn't want to hear me complain about my pain, stress, or frustration. Really, nobody did. Who would? In my sullen mind, Scott's request to "just be happy" was merely a dismissal of my emotions or any of the reasons behind them.

Even if he had good intentions and wanted me to feel better, to show me he loved me no matter what, I hated that he told me to "just be happy." There was no happiness switch. That was impossible. *Does he want me to pretend none of this is happening and just fake a smile?* I had no energy left to put on a show for him. How could I possibly worry about pleasing him when I was drowning in survival mode and felt like stress was suffocating me?

The problem was that it was happening to both of us and neither one knew how to help the other. He needed to decompress from his day, just like I did. Instead of meeting one another somewhere in the middle, we were just bumping into one another's overworked, stressed-out mind and body. We were both too exhausted to figure out how to change that.

Sugar was my escape, reward, and best friend. It was the one thing I could count on to make me happy, even if it was just for a moment. Right alongside the chocolate chip cookies or ice cream, I stuffed all my emotions down in some dark, unseen place that I'd ignore. Sometimes at night, while Scott was watching a movie with the girls, I'd sneak off in my car all alone. I'd drive to Friendly's, park, and walk up to the takeout window, glancing over my shoulders to see if anyone was watching.

"I'll have a Reese's Peanut Butter Cup sundae with extra peanut butter sauce." Saliva pooled up in my mouth with anticipation of my first bite.

As soon as the heavenly union of fudge and peanut butter hit my tongue, my body quivered with ultimate delight. *I deserve this*, I thought. Alone, I sat in my car, groaning with pleasure at each gratifying morsel. Relaxing, entitled indulgence.

Although I didn't want to admit it, I needed help. Something inside of me was whispering to me, nudging me to get that support and guidance. It was a loving voice, one I wanted to listen to. I had never been to therapy, but I decided maybe I should give it a try. I called Dr. Altman to ask for a recommendation.

"I think I need someone to talk to. Can you recommend a therapist for me?" I confided in her. I told her how I had never felt this way before in my life, so out of control and helpless.

The first therapist on the list was not a match for me. As I watched him with his one leg crossed over the other, pad of paper on his lap, I could see that even though listening was his profession, he was solution-oriented, and I wasn't looking for a solution. There was no solution. I wanted to release emotion and get validation that yes, it sucked, and no, I wasn't crazy.

His advice was for me to take a break, a timeout. He recommended I get out of the house during Kelly's therapy, as if taking a trip to the bookstore or getting a manicure would make it easier to walk back into the muck when I returned home. In my mind, he missed the point. I wasn't trying to avoid the mess. I wanted to find a way to deal with it more effectively. I needed to dig deeper, not run away.

The second therapist I went to understood exactly where I was coming from. This time around, I didn't have to explain the situation or defend my frustration. She just got it. Her expertise was helping families deal with autism and other special needs. A perfect fit.

Her gentle, loving expression and undivided attention absent of any agenda instantly put me at ease. She listened with her whole body, not just her ears. I sat in one corner of the dark-brown leather couch with my feet crossed at the ankle. Relaxing into the moment, I allowed my head to rest on my hand that was propped up by the arm of the couch. I felt safe to share the frustration of autism and its effect on all of us. Mostly, I talked about Kelly, but I also expressed my worry about her sister, how was autism affecting Natalie. How could I control Kelly's seemingly uncontrollable behavior?

The lack of sleep, the overwhelming and consuming distraction of Kelly's hyperactivity, her inability to focus, her tendency to hit, throw tantrums, and steal things from Natalie's room, and the sensory issues—I went through the rest of the list. I recounted the broken record of fears and frustrations that'd been running on a loop in my mind for many months. I talked about chores that drained me as if a clean house or folded laundry were measurements of accomplishment. I shared my loneliness and how it seemed that no one understood the depth of the situation.

If you have cancer, a life-threatening disease, people flock to express concern and offer donations of support. But with autism or mental health issues, people run away as if it's contagious. They don't know how to help. I get that it's difficult to approach the unapproachable. The words flowed freely out of my mouth like a river after a heavy rain.

At the end of my very first session, the therapist asked me what I was feeling.

"Hopeful," I answered. "Hopeful that Kelly will get better."

I answered as if this were a sickness that improves with medicine and time. The therapist knew more than me. I was ignorant and oblivious to the fact that autism would be a lifelong disorder Kelly would struggle to deal with and that she may never be safely independent.

Over time, without realizing it, I let my guard down. The therapist always paused after asking me a question, granting me time to ponder, explore. Her dark-brown eyes and soft smile invited me to go deeper, be free, be myself. She hugged a mug of tea in her hands as if we were friends sharing the trenches of parenting in my kitchen. Like chipping away stone in a sculpture, the therapist woke me up to the profound loss I was overlooking—the loss of all the dreams and expectations for us as parents and for our beautiful daughters, because they were both affected by the pervasive nature of autism.

These sessions helped me get back in touch with my feelings and relearn how to name them. I had become numb in order to protect and help Kelly. Because of her inability to process language and interpret others' emotions, I forced myself to become silent, stoic, and stuffed my feelings away as if they were not nearly as important as hers.

Eventually, by granting myself permission to feel loss, I was able to find the bright side. Yes, we'd be challenged probably forever, but I was able to find the beauty in letting go of all expectations and surrendering to simply loving Kelly.

Therapy helped me wake up and shift my perspective. In turn, that transformation opened me up to looking at my health and eating in a new way, a loving and accepting way. The next step in taking charge of my body and mind flowed naturally. On my own, I decided to address my lifelong tummy troubles by going gluten-free. I don't know why I picked gluten first, but I did. It was pure instinct. I guess I just figured I'd follow Kelly's lead.

Maybe it sounds silly, but I'll never forget the day. On a sunny, crisp fall morning in 2002, while the girls were at school—Kelly in kindergarten and Natalie in second grade—I was enjoying a quiet morning home by myself. I stood at the kitchen sink, staring out the window, captivated by the dim sunlight hitting the trees in our yard. *I can do this. I want to do this.* Because I'd already committed to making and buying gluten-free foods for Kelly's required diet, I figured it couldn't be that hard for me to eat that way, too.

After I'd sipped my morning cup of tea, I drove twenty minutes to the health food store where I got all of Kelly's gluten-free foods. Alone, I took my time perusing the shelves to see if there were any new products to try or ones I'd been overlooking with Kelly by my side. When we went together, I had to be quick. But that day, on the first day of my gluten-free adventure, I was relishing in the freedom to make my own choices, to relax into this new way of life.

I loaded up my cart with Kelly's favorites and some intriguing new ideas for either her or me like ginger snap cookies, English muffins, and quinoa pasta. So far, we'd only tried brown rice noodles, and though Kelly ate them, they were a little too sticky for my taste. Buttered noodles had always been a favorite, easy meal when I was growing up and when the girls were little. Since Natalie wasn't gluten-free, I kept a box of regular pasta on hand at all times for her. Meanwhile, Kelly adjusted to the gluten-free noodles topped with tomato sauce instead of butter.

Thanks to my prior initiation with Kelly, going gluten-free was surprisingly painless and simple. I bought a binder to put all my favorite recipes in and printed out lists of foods that were gluten-free.

Meats and veggies were already usually gluten-free so that was easy. Baked potatoes were a new favorite side dish, especially when eating out at a restaurant like the Outback Steakhouse where they coated the potato with oil and salt before baking it, turning it into a delicious and savory treat.

At home, at least once a week, dinner was simply a baked potato with veggies. Scott loved baked potatoes, so it was a quick and effortless meal. We ate ours with butter. Kelly ate hers plain with lots of salt. Rice was another straightforward, simple option. It only took twenty minutes to cook and everyone in my house liked it. With the leftovers, I'd make fried rice with oil, eggs, and frozen peas or broccoli.

Homemade granola was my go-to breakfast. I used the recipe from Ina Garten's *The Barefoot Contessa Cookbook* and made it with gluten-free oats, sunflower seeds, slivered almonds, coconut, walnuts or pecans, honey, and oil. Every morning, in a bowl, I combined plain, unsweetened Stonyfield Farms yogurt, sweetened with a little fresh-squeezed orange juice, with a scoop of granola. Or, I'd make scrambled or fried eggs with a side of fruit. Kelly didn't like the granola. For breakfast, she ate gluten-free By George English Muffins or Van's Natural Foods waffles.

Beer and pizza. That's what I missed most. Traditionally, Friday nights were a night off from cooking. Scott and I used to sit on the sofa in our sunroom and eat pizza, drink beer, and watch a movie. Being gluten-free meant I couldn't indulge in either of those things anymore. Despite the letdown, I was committed to Kelly and to myself. I'd made myself a promise that we were going to feel as good as possible, which meant no slipping. Not even one sip of beer or bite of pizza.

Like cheating on a test in school, it would be so easy to glance over at the answers of the brainiac sitting next to me, but the fear of getting caught always stopped me. With gluten, the anxiety over getting sick or going back to being unhappy was what made me not want to cheat. Besides that, once I'd embraced eating gluten-free on my own, I realized Kelly needed me. As her mom, I was driven to lead by example. It had to become a way of being, not just a rule to follow. I had to own it.

Without gluten, my stomach was quiet and calm. The sour acid feeling right under my ribs that made me hungry all the time was finally gone. It no longer woke me up at night, and when I got up in the morning, I didn't have the urge to eat right away. My belly was satisfied and content. The fog that clouded my brain was gone, I was sleeping again, and my improved reasoning and understanding had me thinking quick and clear. In the months that I'd gone gluten-free, I felt like I was waking up from a restful hibernation. For the first time in years, I was refreshed and energized.

Usually, after Natalie and Kelly left for school, I felt emotionally and physically exhausted. Now, instead of wanting to crawl back into bed, I couldn't wait to put on my sneakers, get outside, and run. Without gluten, my legs felt stronger and my lungs breathed easier. I could run farther than ever before.

I had been fighting symptoms related to what I ate my whole life without realizing it. It was one thing to watch the magical transformation in Kelly, but finally feeling good in my own body was the most powerful endorsement of all. Knowing I could change how I felt with my diet was beyond empowering. It was life-changing.

My initial motivation was all about my stomach, and the unexpected outcome was watching the irritability, resentment, anger, and frustration that I'd been shoving down for years marvelously dissipate. Instead of a swirling, impending storm deep inside me, there was a lightness that hadn't been there since I don't know when, maybe ever. Everything seemed sunnier, brighter. Now, I could be happy without having to force it.

Maybe I was programmed from a young age to rely on antibiotics as the quick fix. Growing up, like most in my generation, I was under the impression that antibiotics and prescriptions were the only way to heal pain and sickness. Because of that, I'd unknowingly become conditioned to believe that the little square white piece of paper with a prescription scribbled on it was a gift. Back then, I didn't realize the role I could play in my own health.

All the doctors and specialists I'd been to made the same mistake—they treated each symptom or illness as an island, standing alone in a separate container, when, really, they were all connected.

To me, it was crystal clear. My chronic pain, itchy scalp, tummy troubles, and other annoying symptoms all stemmed from one thing—inflammation in my gut. If I'd known my body needed me to step up and play the principle role in getting better, I would have done it so many years earlier. In addition, my upbringing did not prepare me for my wildly successful transformation at thirty-five years old. Surprised and grateful, I was caught completely off guard.

It's so hard to imagine something you've never felt. I didn't know what it felt like to not be sick. I didn't know how badly I felt until I started to feel better. Once I'd given myself permission to care for my own needs and started paying attention to my body on a more intimate level, there was no turning back. I would become an advocate for my own health by changing what I ate while willingly becoming Kelly's partner. I was starting to see that the journey was about more than just Kelly.

She's not the only one. I know she's really not the only one.

9

pioneering the path

"It's so important to just sometimes listen to yourself, to listen to the voice deep inside you. That voice is usually right so don't ignore it. Listen to it."

Earlier that year, on Memorial Day weekend of 2002, we relocated to a new house across town. The fifteen-year-old home was situated on the corner of a quiet cul-de-sac, across from a park, and walking distance to the elementary school that Natalie and Kelly attended together. It offered the perfect combination of both privacy and convenience. Since the house had a large fenced backyard with a pool plus more livable space for our family and guests, it was a good move for us. Most of all, Scott and I prayed that all the sick, sleepless nights were left behind at our old house. In our minds our new home represented a fresh start.

Even though we were in more of a groove, I was still working hard around the clock to keep the peace. All it took was one teeny-tiny shift in Kelly's diet or supplement regime to set her into a tailspin of regression, anger, and hyperactivity. It was like we were taking three steps forward, two steps back. Things were certainly not perfect, but in my gut, I knew our routine was working. Kelly and I just needed more time.

"You're mean! I don't like the way you look at me!" Kelly blurted out, punching her own thigh with her fist while glaring at Natalie.

"I'm not mean," Natalie retorted, looking down, annoyed with the distraction while she was packing her backpack with home-work from the night before.

"Yes, you are!" Kelly persisted. "And you're mad. Why are you mad, Natalie?" Kelly pushed harder into her own thigh with her clenched hand.

Kelly was confused by her sister's blank expression, narrow gaze, and quiet concentration as Natalie stood next to the kitchen table making sure she had everything she needed for school before eating breakfast. Natalie was not laughing, and she was not angry. Instead, she was deep in deliberate thought. Kelly misinterpreted these pensive expressions.

"I'm not mad," Natalie clarified. "This is mad!" she finally gave in, sticking out her tongue and making her eyes bulge in Kelly's direction.

In the mornings before school, there was always an argument between the two of them, typically starting with one of Kelly's outbursts and inability to grasp time. Natalie would try to help out, warning Kelly that she had fifteen minutes to get ready before we'd be leaving for school, which meant nothing to Kelly.

Not only were transitions difficult, shifting from one part of the day to the next, but so was the concept of time. Rushing and, conversely, waiting idly were two things that confused and aggra-vated Kelly. Mornings were always about rushing. Complicating the issue even more was that Kelly needed a few extra minutes to process spoken language and what was happening around her, something many of us take for granted.

These mornings, which I could only hope would start to get better by the time the girls got a little older, were absolute may-hem. Most days, I shed tears of helpless frustration once they were safely at school.

In the fall of 2003, Natalie was in fourth grade, a model stu-dent, at the top of her class, and in the gifted program. She looked forward to getting up and going to school. Learning excited her.

Kelly, a first-grader, openly hated school, which she'd tell me every day. Even though they were at the same school, in the same building, with the same hallways, classrooms, and teachers, their experiences could not have been more different. Natalie was an independent learner, and an easygoing, naturally gifted student who enjoyed a well-rounded education. Kelly, on the other hand, required a lot of dedicated, undivided attention, and we were learning every day what "undivided" really meant.

Still, because Kelly was starting first grade, it felt like we were at a new beginning. Our mindset was positive and upbeat. She had an IEP (Individualized Education Plan), and we were assured she'd have the accommodations she needed in the classroom. As additional support, one of her therapists would shadow her at school. Regardless if Kelly's experience at school would be "abnormal" by typical standards, we were going to keep moving forward. I was pioneering a path for her, for us.

Over the last two years, we'd made so much headway. With clear direction from doctors we could trust, one DAN conference under our belts, along with countless hours of therapy, we were more confident in where things were heading with Kelly. Kelly still had twenty-eight hours a week of behavioral support with the wraparound therapists and went to both speech and occupational therapy three times a week. I meticulously and religiously followed Dr. Baker's protocol. Kelly had been on antifungal medication to treat her dysbiosis, or yeast overgrowth, for about a year now. While things weren't necessarily resolved, they seemed less erratic.

Gluten-free had become a way of life for Kelly and me. We'd found our substitutes and, thankfully, Kelly was accepting of her limited but safe options. Every now and then, an accidental slip reminded us of its effectiveness. One Sunday, Kelly accidentally ate a slice of regular bread. Yes, the kind full of gluten, and it sent her into a weeklong bout of sickness. Another time, it was hot dogs. It became exhausting to expect precision and end up with disaster, but we tried to remain calm. This composure came with accepting that we were settling for very gradual, slow progress.

Fully dedicated to the journey of understanding Kelly's condition, constantly educating myself, doing research, and discussing her symptoms with all her therapists and experts in autism, I was beginning to appreciate that her behaviors and tantrums were symptoms of some sort of imbalance in her body, a sickness that accompanied autism. All I could do was accept that this was what we had to deal with.

It was obvious to me that Kelly was acting out of pain, discomfort, or confusion, but the world around us did not have the same understanding. The other moms in the supermarket or at school glared at Kelly's reactions, and it seemed that teachers at her school did too. In other words, to outsiders, Kelly just looked like a spoiled, stubborn brat.

"You know, when Kelly gets that, um . . . ," her teacher hesitated to tell me, "attitude?"

The teacher blamed Kelly's struggles in the classroom on the obstinate temperament she observed, completely dismissing the fact that Kelly's learning challenges, behaviors, and disposition all stemmed from her disorder: autism.

Given all I'd learned about autism, in my gut, I knew better. But I also understood it was complex. Even I'd forget the nuances of autism every now and then. I'd let my frustration get the best of me, forgetting Kelly's lack of authority over her reactions. To remind myself, I'd write lists down on paper, place sticky notes on the wall of my closet and inside the kitchen cabinets. A five-by-seven-inch spiral notebook was by my side at all times. I took voracious notes to document suspected triggers and the types of behavior they'd bring about. Both Dr. Baker and Robin suggested this behavior-tracking method—one for her supplement protocol, the other for her therapy goals.

One day, as the three of us were walking from the car into the hospital for Kelly's occupational therapy, Natalie brushed by Kelly, knocking her shoulder against her sister's. Treading behind them, I watched it happen.

"Natalie!" I called out, trying to avoid a meltdown right before Kelly's appointment. "Don't push your sister," I demanded, wishing Natalie would understand that it was not a good time to pick a fight.

"I didn't do anything," Natalie snapped back at me. "This would be pushing my sister!" She bumped into Kelly harder as they walked down the hallway to the waiting room. Kelly started crying, and I stepped between the two of them before Kelly could hit Natalie.

"Go sit in the waiting room," I barked at Natalie, my eyes bulging and the muscles in my neck tightening. I was trying not to make a scene, but we'd already made one. Once they were separated, Kelly calmed down and went along with the occupational therapist for her appointment. I made my way back to the waiting room where Natalie was sitting in one of the chairs, staring up at the television. She avoided looking at me at first, her whole body stiff.

"How come I'm the only one who ever gets punished?" Natalie interrogated me as I sat next to her. "Kelly never gets punished," she blurted out.

I didn't know how to respond. From her perspective, she was right. It looked like Kelly was rarely reprimanded. Sometimes Kelly yelled fifteen to twenty times in an hour and didn't get disciplined once. Not sure what to say, I sat in silence while my stomach ached. Besides, there was no need to reply to Natalie immediately. She knew I didn't have an answer.

One of the problems was that I didn't think Kelly understood consequences, and she was excessively impulsive. Rules meant nothing to her. So, to Natalie, it looked like I favored Kelly when really, I didn't. Or, wait, maybe I did. Maybe I did because I needed to. Conflicting voices bounced back and forth in my head.

"Why does everything have to be about Kelly?" Natalie whimpered, breaking the silence. Natalie was weary too. I could see it.

She tried not to complain, but she didn't know how else to express the bottled up frustration and anger. I attempted to give Natalie my undivided attention at least once a day, but it was not enough. My mind was always preoccupied with Kelly.

"It's just the way it is. I wish I could make it better, but I can't," I finally conceded, trying to console her, fighting back the tears. My urge was to hug her tight, but I was afraid she would push me away. Instead, I just placed my hand on her thigh and left it there for a few seconds.

How could I tell Natalie that we expected more from her than Kelly without hurting her feelings or making her resentful? A bright child, I knew she could fully comprehend rules and demands. *Does she not understand Kelly has autism and what that means?* I wondered and thought that maybe Natalie needed more education on why Kelly acted the way she did. But I feared if I explained that, it would only look like I was defending Kelly.

A few months later, Kelly was home sick. It was a cold winter morning and with a hot mug of tea in my hands, I watched out the kitchen window as Natalie walked alone to school, carrying her backpack, viola, and lunch box. I stared at Natalie's powder-blue ski coat, hoping she was warm enough. *I'm sorry. I never wanted it to be like this,* that voice inside me whispered. I hoped that message would make it to her and that she'd understand. Then, suddenly, Natalie's feet slipped on a patch of ice on the sidewalk and she fell down. I wanted to go running to her, but she quickly got back up and kept walking to school, independent, hardened and strong.

Tears streamed down my face. All morning I just sat and cried, worrying that I'd neglected Natalie at some point, that she resented me. I cried because I didn't have answers to a better way. Mostly, I cried because I knew I couldn't fix it. I was trying as hard as I could to make it better, but the weight of autism on our family was never going away.

Despite the fact that the dietary changes, Dr. Baker's antifungal parade, and supplement recommendations showed marked improvement in Kelly's disposition and health, she still engaged in yelling, hitting, and irrational, forgetful thoughts. When I left her to go to the laundry room or kitchen, Kelly would yell for me as if she was lost and unable find her way back home. Like Velcro, she was glued to me and I to her. I knew Kelly needed someone like me to rely on and attach to—all kids do—but I started to question if my unwavering patience and acceptance were leading her astray, if her dependence on me was unhealthy. I asked Robin if there was a way to create some distance, to gently release some of the burdensome attachment.

The book *1-2-3 Magic* detailed a new approach to behavior that Robin taught me. Robin relied on *1-2-3 Magic* for its simplicity and ease of follow-through, recounting how it had a positive impact on all the children she worked with, especially those similar to Kelly. With the way Robin understood Kelly, how Kelly processed language slower (the less words, the better), Robin knew it would be a fit for her. *1-2-3 Magic*'s three-strikes-you're-out approach removed conversation and negotiation from the equation, taking the emotion out of discipline. As soon as a negative or targeted behavior happened, the only thing said was "one" coupled with holding up one finger. Then, when another infraction happened, "two." With "three" came the punishment or consequence—usually a time-out or removal of a preferred activity or toy.

Robin coached me to try it out and, for the sake of consistency, told me to encourage Scott to use it too. She said it would feel almost as if we were speaking a different language. Almost immediately, we saw a dramatic change in response from Kelly when we used it. *Yes!* Finally, she was responding to discipline with a less violent, more understanding attitude, and we could get to a resolution quicker.

When other people engaged in conversation near or around Kelly, she would get extremely agitated and angry at them as if they weren't including her, when, really, she simply couldn't follow along. To help ease her frustration, I learned to try to say as little as possible and to choose my words carefully when in her presence. Since Kelly responded to simple, slow, easy-to-understand language—and this is not the way people are used to talking in the real world—it made sense that Kelly would be more tense, more volatile in public places. It all made so much sense now.

Our public school did not have an autistic support classroom. So, the only option for Kelly in first grade was learning support. Unfortunately, the learning support teacher was not trained in autism, neither from a behavioral perspective nor an academic one. It was a disaster. Every afternoon I walked through the park to meet Kelly and Natalie at the end of the school day, and every day Kelly came running into my arms crying.

After school, Monica, the therapist that shadowed Kelly in the classroom, arrived at our house to work with Kelly. Looking rattled, disapproval gleamed in her protruding eyes. Anxious to tell me some of the mistreatment she'd witnessed in learning support, Monica quickly pulled me aside, away from Kelly.

"That teacher doesn't understand autism," Monica whispered, confiding in me. "It's not fair to Kelly," she empathized, letting out a heavy sigh while gently shaking her head. A few moments later, when she handed me her pen to sign a paper documenting the hours she was at school, I noticed her hands were trembling. Monica's reaction to the situation, being that she was an educated, well-trained professional, was almost more upsetting than witnessing Kelly running out of school crying.

The idea of someone taking charge of my child triggered instinctive anger in me. The notion that a teacher, hired to teach young children using patience and understanding, would try to jam a square peg into a round hole, pushing and pushing even though it didn't fit, made me want to scream and sob all at the same time. I imagined confronting the teacher and envisioned what I'd say to her. *Don't you get it? Why aren't you trying to understand what's behind Kelly's behaviors? Have you ever read a book on autism? Do you even know what it is?*

What baffled me most was why the school wouldn't collaborate with the wraparound agency or use them as a resource. Wouldn't a team approach cultivate more learning and engagement? It didn't work if teachers weren't trained on how to handle idiosyncratic behaviors. I reminded myself over and over that this was not Kelly's fault.

Scott and I had to make a tough decision.

Before the end of first grade, we pulled Kelly out of school. The director of special education agreed that her needs weren't being met and suggested we investigate another placement for Kelly, including visiting other school districts.

At the recommendation of an independent school psychologist, starting in May and for the summer months, Kelly did an intensive learning and reading program called Lindamood-Bell. It was an hour away from our house in Ardmore, a suburb of Philadelphia. How Kelly responded to this type of curriculum would help us determine her placement for the upcoming school year.

Prior to starting at Lindamood-Bell, Kelly showed significant impairment in her underlying capacity to recognize sight words and to spell. Her reading tested below kindergarten level. *Is she capable of learning? Will she be able to read?* Those were the questions we kept asking ourselves as we faced the fork in the road, an undeniable turning point.

In the twelve weeks Kelly was at Lindamood-Bell, five days a week, four hours per day, Kelly learned phonemic awareness and decoding skills. The intensive, one-on-one, direct instruction helped her jump to a fourth-grade reading level as measured on the Woodcock Reading Mastery Test. This was a huge moment to celebrate since her next steps hinged on this outcome.

Because of her significant progress that summer, the Janus

School, which was exclusively for children with learning disabilities, accepted her as a new student for second grade. Scott and I were relieved and grateful that our investment in Lindamood-Bell had paid off. Proud of her accomplishment and excited to continue learning, Kelly was thrilled about going to a new school where they would know how to teach her.

Within a few weeks back to school in the fall of 2004, we were in a routine and I could hardly believe it. A school van came to the house at 6:30 each morning, stopping at the end of our driveway. It waited for Kelly to get on, never leaving without her. With my undivided attention and guidance to get her dressed and fed, she was never late.

Now in second grade, Kelly still didn't know the word autism. The idea of giving her a label felt wrong, limiting, and we didn't want to put her in a box. The momentum she was gaining was building her self-esteem and a solid work ethic, and we didn't want her to ever use her diagnosis as a crutch. Most of all, Scott and I agreed that the concept was too abstract for her at this age with her limited cognitive skills. Robin agreed. At this point, Kelly thought all her struggles came from food allergies.

"Why is Natalie always a good girl and I'm not?" Kelly asked me while we were in the kitchen together. "I hate my allergies!"

"I want to be like you, Natalie," she said to her sister sitting across the table, finishing her homework. "Quiet, like you," Kelly continued.

Natalie smiled. They were best friends when nothing else was getting in the way. These rare, brief moments of the unbreakable sisterly bond showed me that three steps forward and two steps back wasn't so bad after all. We were still moving forward, together.

Kelly was a very complacent baby, as shown by her willingness to wear her first pair of sunglasses at seven months old.

Scott holding Kelly up high. He had wonderful visions for his precious baby girl.

Me with Kelly at thirteen months old.

Big sister love. Natalie and Kelly on Thanksgiving Day, 1997.

Natalie being creative in the room off our kitchen while Kelly tried drawing with a crayon.

A sweet mother daughter moment in Florida, Easter of 1999. Kelly sitting in her favorite position.

A family portrait on Surfside Beach, Nantucket.

One of Kelly's dress-up moments, wearing her Mary Poppins scarf.

Kelly taking a turn at the lectern in Sconset Chapel after her cousin's baptism in August, 1999.

Kelly building one of her Barbie set-ups.

As vice president of her class, Kelly at the podium again, making the opening remarks at graduation.

Kelly on the bright side, summer of 2015.

10

stronger together

"Keep shining bright and never let anyone take away your light."

By the end of 2004, Kelly was eight years old and had been a patient of Dr. Baker's for two years. The range of medicines we'd tried up to this point was long—tryptophan, melatonin, probiotics, chelation creams, multivitamins, B12 shots, antifungal medication, Actos, betaine, magnesium, calcium, milk thistle, enzymes, and more supplements with fancy names I couldn't spell or pronounce.

The strangest members of her treatment regimen were the chelation creams that Dr. Baker prescribed—glutathione, TTFD (Thiamine TetraHydrofurfuryl disulfide), and DMPS (2,3-Dimercapto-1-propanesulfonic acid). They were compounded by a pharmacy, placed in a syringe, and shipped to our house. With a disposable latex glove on my hand, I'd apply drops of the cream to her forearm and rub it in at alternating times, days, and amounts according to Dr. Baker's instructions. He told us the creams served to pull out toxins or heavy metals believed to be affecting her gut health, mood, memory, and brain functioning. If I didn't keep track of each application, each medication, each appointment on a calendar and in my notebook, I would have lost my mind.

The TTFD cream made Kelly smell like a skunk. Sadly, that's not an exaggeration. Kelly couldn't smell it, luckily, but everyone else could. Her teacher complained about its intensely offensive odor, requesting that we not use it on school days. But I insisted Kelly keep using the cream because she was more calm and focused with it. At all costs, we clung tight to anything that offered even the slightest glimpse of improvement.

Every other month, I had a conference call with Dr. Baker, and then we also had semiannual appointments at his office with Kelly. For her next visit to Dr. Baker, the whole family came along. His office had moved from Connecticut to Sag Harbor, NY, making it somewhat convenient to stop there on our way home from Nantucket. It made me happy to know that this time we could all be there in support of Kelly, and I was excited for Natalie and Scott to experience Dr. Baker's enthusiasm and unwavering confidence in Kelly's progress.

Natalie, Kelly, Scott, and I sat on the couch while Dr. Baker told us a story about one of his patients, a teenage girl similar in many ways to Kelly except that she hadn't spoken a single word in her life. And then a miracle happened. She went on the Specific Carbohydrate Diet (SCD) and words effortlessly spilled out of her mouth.

In awe of her transformation, it was one of the many reasons why Dr. Baker recommended the diet. He explained that, at its core, the SCD served to heal the gut. In his opinion, this was what Kelly needed. A strong advocate of the diet, he'd discussed many success stories with other doctors at the recent DAN conference, and he encouraged us to try it. Desperate and eager for our own miracle, we said yes. That same desperation forced me to blindly overlook how hard it might be.

The SCD would take gluten-free one step further by eliminating all grains and sugar. That was how Dr. Baker explained it. This aligned perfectly with his antifungal protocol. He pointed out that cutting out sugars and starches would starve the yeast, the bad bacteria in Kelly's gut, and thus the healing would continue at a new, hopefully faster pace. Without changing the foods she ate, the vicious cycle would merely continue. Hence the name of the book, *Breaking the Vicious Cycle.*

"Read the book," Dr. Baker instructed me, writing down the name of the author and creator of the diet, Elaine Gottschall. "It explains everything and has all the lists of what to eat and what not to eat." I was dying to know more and wanted to start immediately but had research to do first. I gave myself some time to figure out our next steps.

Once the girls went back to school, I ordered *Breaking the Vicious Cycle* from Amazon. I spent every free moment on SCD patrol, learning as much as possible. I read and reread the book, trying to grasp the concept of how restricting certain types of foods would heal the gut. It echoed things I'd learned from Dr. Baker and at the DAN conference but got into more detailed explanations. The book was loaded with nuggets of information that cemented my commitment and ignited my passion for our upcoming journey.

One of Elaine's statements stuck out, reverberated in my brain, energizing my promise to follow the diet: "Instead of considering these illnesses hopeless, it is preferable to consider the majority of psychoses (like autism) as reactions to biological factors which are very often digestive in origin."

Elaine's descriptions of the science behind the diet fascinated me. On the SCD, the chemical structure of the foods dictated whether or not they were allowed. For example, the only carbohydrates permitted were monosaccharides. These consisted of real (not canned) fruit, honey (particularly raw honey), and most vegetables. With illustrations and scientific explanations, Elaine described how their simple molecular structure facilitated absorption in the intestines more easily.

Carefully and thoroughly, Elaine expounded on how disaccharides and polysaccharides were not permitted, including grains, sugars, milk, and processed cheeses. It was all new to me. Lactose and most sugars are disaccharides made of two molecules, whereas starches like potatoes, corn, rice, and wheat are polysaccharides with multiple molecules strung together. I wrote down her examples and reasons furiously in my notebook: *The more complex the molecule, the harder it is to digest. Complex carbohydrates are not easily digested, and therefore, they feed the harmful bacteria in the gut.*

I couldn't download the new information fast enough. The more I reiterated the facts in my brain, the more I became a gut health junkie. There wasn't a lot of information online, but enough to boost my confidence. Most of the kernels of inspiration came from one site called Pecan Bread, written by mothers of children with autism following the diet. It explained the stages of the diet with charts of what to eat and recipes organized by those stages and ingredients. For example, even though some dairy was permitted on the diet, there was a section for dairy-free recipes, which was perfect for us since Kelly needed to be dairy-free.

Like Dr. Baker mentioned, I learned that the SCD is most often used to treat gut disorders like Crohn's disease, ulcerative colitis, celiac disease, diverticulitis, and chronic diarrhea. It sounded like the perfect remedy for Kelly.

Before studying the SCD, I hadn't really grasped celiac disease or how important a gluten-free diet was for healing, not just for managing symptoms. Now it made perfect sense. If someone with celiac disease eats gluten, the immune system kicks into gear, mounting an attack on the invader (gluten). This affects the constitution of the gut and its delicate balance of flora.

These attacks damage the tiny but important villi lining the small intestine that are responsible for absorbing the nutrients from food. Once those fragile villi are damaged, the person with celiac faces nutritional deficiencies. This so perfectly explained what was going on with Kelly. Her bony limbs screamed for nourishment, and her distended belly was fermenting all the food she couldn't digest.

For the diet to work and initiate healing, Elaine made it very clear that the SCD required a full commitment. That meant 100 percent adherence to the legal list of foods and 100 percent avoidance of the illegal ones. Cheating or eating the wrong foods, even a little bit, would cause inflammation and cloud the picture. I imagined it was just like how picking a scab causes scarring or itching poison ivy makes it spread, delaying recovery.

I was viewing the SCD as an experiment. What did we have to lose? Besides, I really wanted to know if the diet would make a difference for both of us. If we didn't do it, we would never know.

Given all the facts, the most manageable way to deal with initiating the SCD was to move into it slowly. Already October, I decided that since it'd be too difficult to introduce such a radical shift during the holidays, we'd start in the new year. I used that time to create my game plan—what were we going to eat, what would our daily meals look like, what food would each meal require, and where would I buy that food? I got my answers. I made my plans. Once I had all my ducks in a row, I was excited to begin the process of healing in both our guts. In addition to the possibility of healing, being Kelly's partner was a huge element of my motivation.

For our start date, I picked a weekend—the second Saturday in January 2005. New year, new plan. To prepare Kelly, I told her weeks ahead of time and reassured her that we'd be a team, eating the same foods together. Explaining it to her and having her agree to give it a try helped me feel energized, ready. The fact that I was doing it with her made her more comfortable with our new routine. She trusted me. Because the specifics were hard for her to comprehend, I kept my explanations simple, to the point. To boost her compliance, I focused on what we could eat, not on what we were avoiding.

In that early stage, it was the promise of healing that I really relied heavily on. I harped on this point when I presented the SCD diet to Kelly.

"If we follow the plan, then you will get better. It will help make your tummy troubles go away. And maybe one day, you won't have so many allergies. That's why we are doing it."

Over and over again throughout the day, I repeated the goal in my mind: we were healing ourselves with what we put into our bodies. I invited this new encouraging mantra into our daily routine. If we didn't change what we ate, our bodies would be stuck in the same vicious cycles. If she ate sugar, she'd just be feeding the bad bacteria and yeast in her gut, and she'd never get better no matter what medication she took. Medication was merely a Band-Aid, not a cure. The SCD had the promise of a cure.

Everything we ate had to be made from scratch—no canned tomatoes, no cold cuts, no mayonnaise or ketchup. No more gluten-free Van's Natural Foods waffles, By George English Muffins, Nature's Path Crispy Rice Bars, Pamela's cookies, Rice Dream ice cream, rice milk, or rice protein powder. French fries and potatoes were also out since they were illegal. The only legal sweetener was honey—no stevia, no agave, no sugar (brown, white, or raw), and no maple syrup.

The first stage of the diet was comprised of very bland foods that were easy to digest. There were only a few options like eggs, chicken, beef, turkey, homemade chicken soup, gelatin, and select vegetables. I told myself we'd take it day-by-day, meal-to-meal. Just like when I got back into running after months off, I'd coach myself to ease back into it, step-by-step. I managed my expectations and energy for slow, steady success. It made sense to handle the new diet the same way.

So, on that first day, I woke up and soon after brushing my teeth and getting dressed, Kelly was awake and ready for breakfast. I scrambled two eggs in some olive oil for her because she couldn't have butter or dairy. Even though eggs were on her "avoid" list from the food sensitivity testing we did with Marilyn, I still gave them to her because I didn't know what else to feed her for breakfast. Sure enough, she threw up. Not a good start.

The next day, I made sausage from scratch with ground pork, Italian seasoning, garlic, salt and pepper. Kelly ate a few bites before sticking out her tongue and saying, "Yuck!" Visually, none of the new recipes I cooked were appealing to Kelly because they were such a big shift from what she was used to seeing— preformed sausage patties, meatballs, hot dogs, perfectly shaped waffles, and cookies. When I made meatballs from ground turkey for dinner, Kelly took one look and then said she wasn't hungry. With her first bite of Applegate gluten- and dairy-free hot dogs, she spat the skin out.

Whenever Kelly would refuse to eat more than just a few nibbles of her meal, her complaints included fearful claims that the particular food was going to make her choke. She'd declare, "I can't swallow that!" while pushing her plate away. The way she scrunched up her nose at the smell or look of the food and then persisted to protest until tears welled up in her eyes, I could tell this was a real fear for her. But how could I get her to eat? It was just like potty-training. There was no forcing her.

While I was fixated on the rules, Scott understood Kelly needed some "selling." At mealtime, his tactic was to market the food to her by describing how delicious it was as he ate it in front of her. Father and daughter, they sat next to each other on stools at the kitchen counter, the knees of his six-foot-six frame hitting the island cabinet. He used his humor and charm to distract her, and then he convinced her the food tasted good even if it didn't look like it. To show her we weren't poisoning or punishing her, he'd always take the first bite.

"Yum, this is good! And Mom made it special for you," he would say, beaming with approval, licking his lips and glancing over at me with a loving sparkle in his eye. Sometimes it worked and sometimes it didn't, but the game was bringing them together for a good cause. I watched from my end of the island with grateful pride at the way Scott rallied behind my efforts on behalf of Kelly. Later, when Kelly wasn't able to hear us talking, I'd thank Scott, and we'd share the frustration of her pertinacious objections.

There were definitely times, even several days at a time, in that first week when I considered giving up on the SCD. I was annoyed by the effort it took to buy new foods, follow the legal list, and make so many recipes from scratch that Kelly refused to eat. Sometimes, I totally understood where she was coming from, and other times, I wanted to scream. *For crying out loud, just eat it!*

When I was really fed up, I even imagined myself holding her mouth open and pouring the food right down her chute, something effortless and quick. Meanwhile, the dishes piled up in the sink because I cooked several different recipes all at once for every meal. *Meal-to-meal*, I'd repeat to myself. That's how we'd get there.

And getting there sure did take time—a lesson we'd already learned from the past. Unfortunately, Kelly and I started to feel worse before we felt better. After the first week of following the diet 100 percent of the time, flu-like symptoms settled into my body. My muscles felt heavy and tired, my bones ached, and my entire body felt weak. I had a queasy feeling in my stomach which left me with little to no appetite, at least for the food I was allowed to eat. Kelly was grumpy, tired, and throwing more tantrums. It was like she was regressing to the body she had before we eliminated her food sensitivities and went gluten-free.

Was it possible that I was leading us down a dark path, onward into the scratchy brush? What had I done? Was I crazy? I scolded myself: *Why are you doing this? You are just making her more sick!* Again, I wondered if this new "magical" solution was really worth it.

I scheduled a conference call with Dr. Baker to discuss our challenges with the diet and to get some support around this bump in the road. He started by describing the process of digestion to me. Digestion was something I'd never really thought about. I cared more about how my food tasted than where it was going or what my body was going to do with it. But now, with this experiment on my body and Kelly's, I was paying attention. Dr. Baker spelled it out like this: When poor digestion persists, which it often does since it's a subtle thing most people don't think about, then toxic bacteria grows in the intestines. This was what he would refer to as the "bad guys." Following the SCD would address this imbalance.

Dr. Baker reiterated the reasons for following the diet by pointing out how what we were feeling was a normal result of what he called "die off." Removing starches and sugars, the main thrust of the SCD, starved the "bad guys"—yeast, candida, parasites, bacteria—in the gut, making them "die off." And, there were temporary side effects from these dying pathogens like brain fog, muscle aches, headaches, exhaustion, and dull appetite.

Now, that made sense and reassured me that we were, in fact, doing the right thing. I needed to hear that all of our symptoms, which felt like weakness and failure, were actually signs of healing.

With this insightful information, I had a renewed boost to keep going. Kelly and I committed to each other to stick it out for two more months. If she doubted or protested, I always reminded her of what Dr. Baker said: that we were healing. Her trust in me and our gradual change in mood was pushing us forward, even if it was hard work. I kept telling myself this was a marathon, not a sprint.

Kelly didn't complain every day, but I could tell by the food left in her lunchbox when she came home from school that she was not happy with her choices. Whether the food didn't taste good or she was embarrassed, she wouldn't specify, but I felt like I'd failed her. The options were so limited, and I had very little to work with. I'd pack sliced roasted chicken, a muffin, some almond butter, and water. Sometimes I'd throw in a few carrot sticks, but she'd never eat them. Without enough food, I worried her blood sugar would plummet and bring on tantrums, hitting, or spiraling emotional reactions. Furthermore, I didn't want food to become an emotional battleground between the two of us. I wanted to go back to Goldfish and Oreos, or simply cook something she would eat without having to convince her. Even rice would be nice.

Most days, no sooner would I finish preparing one meal than I'd start to panic over what the next one would be. It was even more overwhelming knowing there were no shortcuts, no bread for sandwiches, no more pasta, chicken fingers, cheese sticks, or pizza. No takeout or fast food restaurants. In fact, we didn't eat out at all on our new plan—it was too difficult to navigate.

Dr. Baker referred to all the moms of his patients as "doctor moms." As doctor moms, we were all determined to find answers for our sick kids and were united by the DAN approach. Being part of this group of perseverant and compassionate mothers gave me the validation and encouragement to continue to explore the organic root causes of Kelly's behaviors and symptoms. I was starting to gain confidence in my ability to listen to and trust my own instincts and to see that they were aligned with something greater than my own anxiety and drive to save Kelly.

Online, in a group forum, I would chat with the other "doctor moms" about the SCD and the various protocols we were following for our kids. This is where I turned for all my advice on the diet, it was my checking point. When it seemed like I was doing it all wrong, I got reassurance to continue.

A few of the doctor moms who were further along offered helpful perspectives based on their own observations and experiences. "It takes a year. Even though there are ups and downs every few months, once you reach the year marker, things will become more stable, consistent, and predictable. The year mark is the magical moment." That was my light at the end of the tunnel, if Kelly and I could just hang in there a little longer.

Elaine Gottschall often commented on our online forum with answers to technical diet questions like why chickpeas, xanthan gum, or stevia were illegal. She empathized with the challenge of how hard it was to implement the diet, having created and done it herself with her daughter. One day I read a post by Elaine where she recommended enlisting some help in the kitchen. "Hire a cook or dishwasher and get your family on board," she wrote. I'd never considered that. I made the mistake of thinking I could be Super-mom—tackling the SCD for Kelly and me while also still cooking separate meals, that included the illegal stuff, for Natalie and Scott.

Interestingly, I was the only mom in Dr. Baker's group who was doing the diet along with my child, 100 percent committed that every morsel that hit my mouth was acceptable, legal SCD food. Everyone else was just doing it *for* their child, not *with* them. When we shared stories on the forum, it seemed like feeding Kelly was more challenging, mostly because she had a larger number of food sensitivities than the other children, the most difficult being eggs. While I felt connected to the group, I needed help beyond what they could offer—I needed someone to talk to, someone to listen to the struggle, suggest ideas, and help me craft a plan to keep us moving in the right direction.

On the *Breaking the Vicious Cycle* website, there was information about an SCD counselor—a mom of three boys who was doing the diet for her sons. In a desperate plea for help, I emailed her and we set up a time to talk. In a very casual discussion on the phone, she gave me some perspective on how kids like food to be cool and suggested I pack mini plastic grape juice bottles or juice boxes in Kelly's lunch. Welch's grape juice was one of the few legal juices on the diet. Interesting perspective, I thought. I was so stuck on what Kelly could eat, keeping it "legal" and nourishing, making it cool never even crossed my mind. While we talked, I could hear her boys' voices in the background.

"Can you hold on a minute?" she asked, pausing to help them with homework while also trying to continue our conversation.

Her heart was in it, but I felt like she couldn't fully appreciate my challenge. She didn't charge me and never followed up with any kind of plan, leaving me still wishing I had help—someone to guide me through Kelly's particular sensitivities, likes and dislikes, and offer more options and mouthwatering ideas. It was almost impossible to bake without eggs or butter. Without them, there was not a single recipe for bread, and the muffins and cookies I made all lacked that fluffy, perfectly shaped look or melt-in-your-mouth texture.

Scrounging for options, one day I decided to make coconut milk to put in a smoothie. Canned coconut milk wasn't permitted because it had guar gum in it—an illegal ingredient on the SCD. I put four cups of boiling water and one cup of unsweetened, shredded organic coconut in the blender. When I turned on the blender, the force of the motor running pushed the water up against the lid, making it slip off. The boiling hot water spilled all over my chest, leaving me with a large, red burn mark. *Forget the milk!* I told myself, feeling like the diet was draining every drop of my energy.

With my changing perspective on the SCD and becoming more black and white with how I viewed food, I began to wonder about our eating habits before Kelly and I made the change to the SCD or even to gluten-free. Back then, why had it felt so liberating to feed her junk and let her eat snacks throughout the day? What made that so satisfying? Or was it just because it was effortless that it had more appeal?

I thought back to the cupboard in my childhood home. In those early years, Mom didn't buy or give us a lot of snacks. If she had sweets, she hid them for a special occasion. The withholding made them all the more tempting. But her secret hiding spots weren't so secret. Guessing where they were, at four years old, I snuck off to the kitchen by myself and climbed up on the kitchen counter to find the cookie cabinet. When I got caught, I was scolded and shamed for scouting out a sweet treat.

Whenever we went to visit my grandmother, my mom's mom, she spoiled us with plates of homemade chocolate chip cookies and potato chips, snacks that were never in our house. She lived far enough away, a three-hour drive, that we didn't see her often. The first time my eyes spotted the shiny, turquoise-blue foil bag of Herr's Potato Chips, I immediately grabbed a handful, shoving the chips in my mouth as fast as I could eat them. They tasted so good I wanted to eat the entire bag by myself. Somehow, I equated my grandmother's generous offerings of greasy, salty potato chips and fresh baked cookies with unconditional love—the kind of love I longed to give to my children.

That's what was so hard about the SCD. I decided long ago that I didn't want my girls to ever feel restricted or deprived of love or food. I wanted to feed them normal snacks that they enjoyed and just naturally wouldn't overeat since they could have them at any time. Thus, they would learn to moderate on their own. But as a parent of a child with highly sensitive dietary restrictions, and following the same restricted diet myself, my view of food was changing. I was learning that food isn't able to give us love, acceptance, or understanding—that would have to come from within.

The hardest thing was sugar. Sugar is the devil. Its seductive, sweet smell triggered memories that made it tempting and nearly impossible to resist. Of all the things Kelly and I cut out of our diet, processed sugar was the hardest thing for me to give up. To cope with my feelings of deprivation, I decided the only way I could handle the emotional breakup was if I had substitutes.

Almond flour was the base I used for all of our baked goods and honey was the sweetener. Chocolate wasn't allowed on the SCD, so I resigned myself to making treats without it too. After about a month on the SCD, I finally created a cookie recipe we both liked. The simplest creation ended up being the best—cookies made with almond flour, honey, safflower oil, cinnamon, and baking soda. They tasted nothing like the Toll House cookies

I used to make, but knowing they were the next best thing, I liked them, and so did Kelly. In the afternoon, when she got home from school, I'd have two or three with a cup of tea while she had more like four or five.

Pretty soon, our taste buds got used to our new sweets and I actually preferred their more natural, real taste. Plus, I never got tired or grumpy after eating them, which kept me motivated to stay the course. Whenever I felt intoxicated by the smell of doughnuts first thing in the morning at the grocery store, or the rich sugary smell of icing on a cake, I just told myself that it wasn't real food and therefore, I couldn't eat it.

One of my new favorite indulgences was homemade almond butter. First, I roasted raw almonds in the oven for thirty minutes. Then, I ground them in my food processor with a little oil and salt until the mixture was creamy and fresh tasting with a buttery, roasted nut finish. I ate spoonfuls of it throughout the day whenever I needed energy or my belly felt hollow. As a kid, it was cheddar cheese that soothed and satisfied my belly. I sliced chunks of cheese and ate as much as I wanted without a thought to its fattening nature. Now, it was becoming clear to me that I craved fat. Fat was a calming fuel for my body and always had been. Protein and fat.

Challenged to make more appealing options to pack in Kelly's lunch, I wanted to create more eggless treats that wouldn't crumble as easily as the cookies or muffins. I mixed raw honey with my homemade almond butter and some almond flour, then, using my hands, formed the batter into balls and rolled them in unsweetened coconut flakes. Almond butter truffles: that's what we called them. I kept them in the fridge because when they were chilled they tasted like fudge. Every day in Kelly's lunch box was a small plastic container of four truffles, and every day the container came home empty.

Raw honey was super sweet like sugar. But, as I was learning, it had more depth and flavor than sugar and I didn't need as much of it to be satisfied. With sugar, I couldn't stop and craved it constantly. Honey was different. I got my fix without it sabotaging me.

Another favorite sweet substitute of mine was a mixture I created with pecans, coconut, vanilla, and raw honey. In my mini food processor, I ground all the ingredients until they resembled a gravel-like texture, and then I'd eat it with a spoon like ice cream or pudding, even though it wasn't creamy. Kelly preferred the almond butter truffles, so I always had a batch of them on hand for her. Sometimes, when I had a real hankering for dessert or candy, I made carrot cake or caramels from the *Breaking the Vicious Cycle* book, but they contained eggs and butter, which made Kelly sick. Conscious of her limitations, I tried not to eat them in front of her even if she seemed content with her own choices.

With cooking, I'd always been an avid follower of recipes, a perfectionist, making sure every measurement was precise, every instruction followed. I was afraid to veer outside the lines for fear of failure. Kelly's food allergies and sensitivities forced me to loosen up, break rules, start changing or creating my own recipes. The realization that I didn't need a recipe for everything I cooked was liberating. It was much simpler to just use a few ingredients anyway. I concentrated on bringing out the true flavor of the food and enhancing it with natural ingredients like garlic, lemon, herbs, salt, or spices. Using this basic approach, I discovered that sauces or flour coatings on fish and chicken really weren't necessary after all.

My mind, body, and appearance were all in a state of transformation. After a month or so of deliberately and diligently following the SCD, my friends noticed my face was slimming and saw more definition in the muscles of my arms. "You look amazing!" they'd say. "What are you eating?"

When I revealed my restrictive diet secrets, telling them, "A lot of nuts, especially a lot of almonds," they were shocked. Though in reality, I knew that the healthy fat in the almonds wasn't really what gave me my new look. It was what I wasn't eating that was making the difference. The real reason I looked less puffy and grey was my abstinence from all the inflammatory ingredients like sugar and flour, but I didn't get into that with them.

With definitive progress, I became hyper-attentive to keeping the momentum going. I became obsessed with knowing and controlling everything that went into or touched our food. Cross-contamination from gluten, dairy, or other illegal foods that could send Kelly into a fit or running to the toilet petrified me. I imagined the chemicals, germs, sweat, or crumbs that might end up on our plate whenever someone else handled our food. It made me not want to eat unless I'd prepared the meal.

Mostly, I was afraid that something would set Kelly off and we'd be back where we started or worse. Practically everything Kelly and I ate was organic. My own anxiety drove me to obsess over harmful pesticides, but it was also recommended by Dr. Baker that Kelly avoid them. Fear drove me to be steadfast in my commitment. Even in all the moments of panic and frustration, we didn't give up.

Two months felt like a year, but finally, Kelly and I arrived at a point where we felt cleansed of our old habits. Our taste buds adjusted, we had our routine down and favorite recipes memorized. We may have been eating the same things all the time, but for now, that was okay.

At first, the difference in Kelly happened in subtler ways, but there was no doubt in my mind that change was present. Her disposition was more placid and responsive. Visual alterations showed in her flattened belly and brighter eyes.

The biggest shifts I noticed in myself were that my energy was consistent throughout the day and clarity settled into my daily thoughts. I felt empowered by my own metamorphosis and began trusting my gut to guide me. I reminded myself of every little positive change, appreciating every step in the marathon. There would be blisters and blunders, but I was convinced we needed to stay on the path.

Before we knew it, four months had passed since we'd started the SCD. It was the end of April 2005, and Dr. Baker and my doctor mom friends would all be at the upcoming DAN conference in Boston. Given Kelly's new routine and diet regimen, I decided it would be best if I went by myself. I asked Scott, a bit reluctantly, if he'd mind staying at home to manage Kelly and her diet. Since he rarely cooked, and Kelly hated when anyone but me made her food, I knew it was a big favor to ask.

I needed to go to the conference, though. It was part of my commitment to our healing plan, and I desperately craved the connection with the other moms to fuel my motivation. So we agreed to give it a whirl, Scott reassuring me the entire time that they would be fine. Just to be safe, I left lists of what to feed Kelly and made sure the fridge was stocked with her morning muffins, almond butter truffles, chicken, and any other of her special requests. Besides, it was only a two-day conference. Somewhere in the back of my mind, I knew they'd survive.

During the five hours in my car on the way to Boston, my thoughts drifted in and out of all we'd done and where we were. It was precious time alone that granted me the space to feel proud of us.

As I exited the Mass Pike onto a road that led to the hotel hosting the DAN conference, I followed a Volvo station wagon with two women in it. Once in the hotel parking lot, I parked my car next to theirs and walked behind them into the conference registration. My goal for being there was to connect with as many people as possible, so I introduced myself and we began talking. One of them, Jennifer, worked for the Jacobi Medical Center in New York City. Jennifer told me about how she considered her son practically fully recovered from autism. I was in awe.

"He has an extraordinarily good diet. He eats a lot of vegetables, especially the dark leafy greens like collard greens and kale," she commented proudly and with levity in her voice, knowing it was not so easy to get an autistic child, or really any child, to eat tough, bitter, chewy greens. As I listened to her stories, I realized there was so much more. I realized there were almost endless options to try before ever considering giving up.

"Check ear wax to see if heavy metals are being excreted," Jennifer instructed me, explaining how she cleaned her son's ear wax daily. She shared more of his regimen including how he got weekly shots of B12, folinic acid, and glutathione IV.

"We get all our supplements tested by independent labs for heavy metal contamination."

She went on to share things I'd never even heard of. Jennifer had a team approach, referring out to several different integrative doctors and methods. One of those doctors was Patricia Kane, PhD.

"She's always been five years ahead of DAN doctors. If you live near Philadelphia, then you need to meet Dr. Patricia Kane," Jennifer advised me.

As fast as my hand would write, I jotted down notes in my notebook while Jennifer rattled off all her resources, successes, and recommendations. Before moving into the conference, Jennifer gave me her business card and invited me to contact her at any time with questions. Her synopsis was more enlightening than anything I heard over the next few hours in the conference room.

Later that night, I met my doctor mom friends in the hotel restaurant. Out of the nearly twenty in the online group chat that I visited daily for SCD advice and commiseration, ten of us were there. Excited to see them live in person, I was hungry to hear more about how others were navigating their child's food allergies, handling resistance to the diet, and adapting the recipes they'd discovered worked well.

One of them struggled with a nut allergy. I empathized with

her, knowing Kelly and I were practically living on nuts between the muffins, almond butter, and cookies we ate every day. She agreed it was hard, but then again, that was his only allergy. He could eat everything else. Many of them cooked with or ate butter and hard cheeses, but Kelly couldn't have dairy. Same with eggs. Baking without eggs really limited our choices. There were substitutes like Ener-G Egg Replacer powder or ground flax seeds mixed with water, but the results were still lacking.

"This is Adam's favorite recipe," said one mom, sharing a lasagna recipe made with cheese, zucchini, sausage, and tomato sauce.

Another shared her brownie recipe: "Have you tried these brownies? They are great for packing in lunch boxes." The brownies were made with eggs and butter. Even though those weren't options for us, I listened anyway, happy to hear their success and hoping maybe it would spark new ideas for me.

Seeing their faces and sharing ideas in person was exactly what I needed. It didn't matter that we all had our own repertoire of favorite recipes based on our children's likes, dislikes, or food sensitivities, we were all in it together. Home alone in my kitchen, overthinking everything in my head, then going online with hopes of finding someone in the same shoes was alienating compared to being here with them.

On the highway driving home, my mind whirled about the conference, all the people I'd met, bonding with the doctor moms, the new ideas, and the referral to Dr. Patricia Kane. She would be closer to us and may very well have an innovative approach to add to our routine. I felt renewed energy and incredible gratitude for those two days in Boston.

When I got home, Kelly hugged me hard and said, "Mom, I'm so glad you're home. Dad doesn't cook like you do."

But they'd done it. He'd stuck to the plan, doing the best he could do, and she'd done her best too. As an added bonus, they appreciated me more than ever. I hugged her back.

"Thanks for following the plan, Kel, even when I wasn't here. I love being your partner and am so glad we're sticking to it together."

With the SCD, Kelly and I leaned on one another to stay committed. She needed me and I needed her. Kelly learned to like the foods I cooked for her, even the muffins that drooped in the middle and crumbled in an instant. The path was ours to forge even if it was vastly different than any other one we'd seen or been on before.

We endured many morning arguments, many dinner compromises, and many bland, boring meals before food started to taste better. Kelly and I were retraining our palates, healing our bodies together. It was anything but a smooth transition, but, side-by-side, we were honoring ourselves and each other. The biggest victory was that Kelly willingly accepted the changes, even if the SCD was hard work and the success was slow.

I knew we couldn't give up. We had to trust that even if we ate the same things over and over or had no choice but to eat a tasteless, boring meal, those foods were healing our bodies. They were what we needed even if they weren't what we wanted to eat. We were still fighting, just fighting in a new ring. Whenever I contemplated quitting, I just thought of Kelly and how I couldn't let her down. I reminded myself of the bigger picture. We were in it for the long haul, for long-term healing and transformation, for the marathon. I'm a fighter and so is Kelly. *We can do this.*

11

in it for the long haul

"Always, always believe in yourself."

When I got my first pair of glasses at age twenty-one, I was shocked at all the detail that I'd been missing. The depth of color, intricate shapes, pointy edges, and sunlight reflecting on every individual tree leaf were things I'd never been able to see before. That same sensation hit me after being on the SCD for about six months. It took a change of scenery for me to notice, but once I did, it became extremely clear what was happening.

It was the end of July of 2005 and after driving for seven hours, we arrived in Hyannis to catch the Nantucket car ferry. The sky was a brilliant, deep blue color, scattered with only a few puffy, pure white clouds. All four of us, Natalie, Scott, Kelly, and I, sat outside on the upper deck of the ferry, our skin warmed by the sun and moistened by the mist of gentle ocean breezes. After two hours, the ferry pulled into Nantucket Harbor. I got up and stood against the boat's protective metal railing, lined with black chain-link fencing.

Looking at the familiar landmarks of Nantucket town—the black face of the clock tower with its shiny gold hands and Roman numerals, the tall, pointy, white church steeple, all the grey shingled buildings—the colors and angles were crisp and clear. The buildings sparkled with light and vibrated an energy that I'd never felt before.

It was a beautiful, sunny summer day, making everything brighter and people happier, but this was about more than just a sunshine serotonin boost. There was a positive shift going on inside my body and brain. The SCD regimen was working for me, it felt right in my body. My lungs welcomed the salt water air and with each breath, I breathed in deeper, feeling the oxygen effortlessly move through my tiny, magical air passages. A warm, relaxed sensation circulated through my body. I was cleansed, weightless.

The ferry slowly passed by Brant Point and the house my family had rented almost twenty years earlier. Memories came flooding back—the carefree days of lying in a bikini on the sand for hours, driving around with Scott, just the two of us, laughing at nonsense in a fire-engine red Jeep Wrangler.

Jolted by the ferry's loud whistle as it approached the dock, I turned around to see Scott sitting with Natalie and Kelly. My lips softened into a faint smile. I was so grateful for him, for our two girls. I was so immensely changed by the love we shared, the love that managed to endure despite our challenges.

It was clear we still had a long way to go, but we were in a groove. Kelly and I were a team, and we had Scott and Natalie's unconditional support. Scott never complained about money spent on strange supplements or doctor's expenses and prescriptions like Lamisil that insurance didn't cover. Our grocery bills were much higher now with our special dietary needs, yet he never said a word about it. His unequivocal blessing allowed me to forge ahead at whatever pace Kelly dictated. Scott could see the progress we were making, and he believed in our plan and in us. He believed in our family.

The experimenting I'd done on my own body allowed me to understand the chemistry behind food so I could identify and accept my own triggers. Feeling it for myself, within my own cells and digestive core, I developed a powerful intuition around how food impacts the body. If I ate a strawberry that wasn't organic, my stomach felt queasy. After a few bites of chicken marinated in soy sauce, I'd get diarrhea. It was the same or worse for Kelly. She regressed with tantrums, lack of sleep, and tummy troubles. Fortunately, Kelly understood if she ate the wrong foods that she'd feel sick. We both knew it just wasn't worth it to deviate from the plan.

I was excruciatingly aware and cautious of sugar, having been addicted to it for years. Thanks to the SCD, I avoided it at all costs. Gluten and grains were also on my radar since they had an impact on my body that was similar to sugar. Even when I ate gluten-free grains like quinoa, I felt lightheaded and had trouble sleeping. Potatoes tasted enticingly sweet and made me crave more and more. According to the SCD, they were illegal anyway, so I eliminated them from my diet. For me, it was easier to be clear, black and white, and avoid those triggers all together.

That's where I really saw my commitment shift into intense passion. If bad food was the only food, I'd rather not eat. If groceries were getting too pricy, I'd find an unnecessary expense to cut out of the budget that month. I didn't need new shoes, I needed my new healthy lifestyle.

Sticking to the SCD structure was paying off in many ways. It was changing the way I viewed food, how food tasted, and what food I craved. I'd always loved salads and even craved them, but I'd also inevitably yearn for a sugar fix after eating a salad. Now, I only craved greens, no sugar. By saying no to the things that grabbed me and yes to those that supported and nourished me, I was honoring myself in a whole new, healthy way.

Like pulling into a new harbor, I was feeling a newfangled freedom—freedom that comes from eating real food, not from eating whatever you want. It dawned on me that I was taking an inside out approach to healing and happiness, and it was working.

I'd found my Zen place, and it happened through changing my diet. My Zen place was a way of being that brought together body, mind, and spirit, almost subconsciously, to create a feeling of inner peace. I realized that I was receiving energy from the foods I ate and saving energy by avoiding the foods that didn't agree with me.

My body knew what it needed, it knew it all along—greens grounded me; protein made me focused and energized. The by-product of this energy and focus was the breakdown of anxiety and stress in my body.

Those toxins that had dominated my reasoning, controlled my entire daily routine—a high-pitched alarm buzzing through my thoughts for so many years—now were hardly noticeable anymore.

One Saturday morning, in the fall of Kelly's first year at Janus, her new school, Kelly gawked at a pink, juicy grapefruit sitting in a bowl on the kitchen counter.

"Mom, can I eat that grapefruit?"

It had been several years since her food sensitivity test reported citrus as a trigger. *Maybe it won't affect her*, I thought to myself before responding. Then, I ran through my mind's food ingredient Rolodex, considering what was in a grapefruit that could harm her. Yes, there was sugar, but it was fruit.

Kelly asked again, and I relinquished: "Sure, you may have it."

Within minutes after eating the grapefruit, anger bubbled up out of her body. She dramatically halted the conversation we'd been having and threw herself on the couch, crying for no reason. Her fists pounded the cushions in protest to an unidentified problem as she mumbled nonsense in between sobs. Then, she quickly ran up to her room and slammed the door. I waited until she calmed down and then went up to talk to her. It was obvious to me, citrus was still a trigger for her, and I wanted to try to gently illustrate that for her.

"Sweetie, do you think it's possible the grapefruit made you feel crazy?" I empathetically probed.

At first she resisted and said, "No, Mom, it wasn't the grape-fruit."

Then I elaborated, reminding Kelly that she had been happy

and calm until she ate it. Then, after eating it, she became angry and upset. I encouraged her to think that perhaps the grapefruit was a trigger for the tantrum, that it wasn't her fault.

"Really, you believe that, Mom?"

"Yes, Kelly. I totally believe it. You showed me it. Besides, remember what we learned about your food sensitivities?"

"No, what about them?" Kelly forgetfully wondered.

"These kind of food allergies aren't just about getting sick. They can also make it hard to sleep, make you sad or mad, and cause tantrums."

"Yeah, I think you're right, Mom," she said, surrendering.

It was a perfect teachable moment for her to feel the reaction in her body and to listen to its message. I desperately wanted her to make the connection so she understood why we ate the way we did, that it was not a form of restrictive torture imposed by her mother. Also, I thought it was important that she know those reactions weren't her fault.

My goal was for her to both comprehend and appreciate the good intentions of choices made for happiness, well-being, and health. Instead of me having to police or direct everything she ate, learning this, feeling it for herself, would be a great way for her to manage her own choices and cope with challenges. Watching her starting to move into this on her own was my greatest reward.

What we were doing wasn't popular or understood by many, but it was working. By following the diet and Kelly's supplement protocol, a positive transformation showed in multiple ways: her sensory issues were significantly improving, she could sleep through the night, her focus sharpened, and she was so much happier. The diet and supplements had a more dramatic impact than any therapy.

With this remarkable healing in Kelly's mind and body, I was caring less and less about looking like a food freak to everyone else. It was such a huge relief to see her feeling better that

I breathed easier, slept more soundly, and walked more lightly. When I coupled that joy with my own metamorphosis, I unabashedly prided myself on our habits.

When I was at a party or out to dinner and the only options were bland, boring foods or nothing at all, I learned to stand strong in my decisions. At restaurants, I'd order steamed vegetables or a plain salad with grilled chicken or beef, and I'd ask for olive oil and lemon to give it a little more flavor. I didn't worry about what other people thought of me or if I was being "rude" to the hostess or waitress. I reminded myself that my choices were about honoring me, and I centered myself in those good intentions. I learned to sacrifice pleasure in those moments for the good of my body.

Though it may have looked like a form of torture to others who ate whatever they wanted, to me, it was a form of loving my body and staying true to what it needed. Plus, I had Kelly at home who was doing the same thing, experiencing the same natural high from just simply feeling good in her body. In being true to our bodies, we were being true to ourselves.

We were very much alone in our choices, though, and I was conscious of it. Running into old friends, they'd comment that I looked great, but it always felt like a backhanded compliment. They'd rave about how much work I was doing to sacrifice myself for Kelly, how selfless I was, but I sensed there was a tinge of judgment in their voices. Even my own parents and Scott's parents questioned our method. Instead of learning more about it or appreciating that this was a move to embrace life and health in a new way, they imagined it was disrespectful, even harmful.

"Come on, have some ice cream," Scott's dad tried convincing me and Kelly. Just like making his bed in the morning, ice cream was a daily after dinner routine in his house.

"No, thank you," I'd politely respond, removing explanation and replacing it with a smile.

In the past, even though I'd repeatedly said it would make her sick, he just couldn't comprehend why Kelly and I didn't eat bread, butter, or ice cream, or how the slightest bit would be a problem. The same was true of my dad.

"I'm worried about you, Suzie. I'm afraid that your way of eating is not social, that it may be perceived as rude," my dad admitted to me while walking together one brisk fall afternoon a few years after I'd been following the SCD.

In my heart, I knew he had good intentions and was just trying to protect me, teach me how to be socially acceptable in the way he'd always done.

"But it's what we need to do, Dad. And it's making me healthier and happier. So I don't care if I'm different." I tried rationalizing my position even though he still didn't seem to understand. He was in denial of Kelly's autism and thought my stomach issues were the same as his. In his mind, he never had to change his diet, so why should I?

Back then, eating the way we did was alienating, but then again, so was autism. Autism wasn't a choice. So the way I saw it, why not be proactive about the things we could choose, like what we ate, even if it was different or unusual? Why not be a pioneer, a leader, and show other people to a better way?

I'd decided that we, as a healthy family, were more important than the judgment and opinions of everyone else around us. Our happiness and well-being were paramount. We accepted that being different was okay if it meant we were being true to ourselves. We didn't have to be like everyone else or make choices based solely on making other people happy at our own cost. We could be authentically us. I say "we" because Kelly trusted me as her partner. She knew I was there for her no matter what and that I wasn't making her do something to control or fix her; rather I was loving her by doing it with her.

My friend, Lisa, tried the SCD with her son, Connor. Even

though they didn't stay on the diet, she was the only one in our town who had any inkling about how we ate or why we were steadfast in those choices. One night, Scott and I took the girls over to Lisa's house for dinner. Even though Kelly and Connor had the same diagnosis, they couldn't have been more different. While Natalie, Kelly, and Connor were in the basement playing together, I went down to check on Kelly. Natalie whispered to me: "Connor's not like Kelly."

Natalie's big, blue eyes widened as she stared at him incredulously. Connor talked a lot, mostly to Natalie, while he bounced on the mini trampoline. Although he was hyper, he was able to focus and engage in a give-and-take manner. Four years younger than Natalie and two years younger than Kelly, Connor was not at all intimidated by his house guests. Instead, he tried to impress them by rattling off facts and asking them to play games.

Kelly didn't play games unless she'd been coached on how to play and had first practiced many times one-on-one. Rules, strategy, and turn-taking were confusing and complex for her at this stage, even if she was eleven years old.

Natalie's friend, Lauren, also had a sibling—a brother—with autism.

When Natalie came home from Lauren's house, she'd say, "Mom, they have no idea. Noah is a piece of cake compared to Kelly. He does whatever his mom says."

I appreciated Natalie's insights, more so than some others I was given. Two of the parents I knew with children on the autistic spectrum—one low functioning and nonverbal, the other high functioning with mostly social issues—frowned at Kelly's tantrums, hitting, and clinging to me. I considered them to be friends, and after all, weren't we all in it together?

I was shocked when one of them, the one whose son was in Kelly's group speech class, preached to me, "Kelly needs to learn to stop hitting."

"Yeah," I mumbled back and looked away, hoping she'd change the subject.

Doesn't she know we're working on that? A knot gripped my stomach, making me queasy and disoriented, just like when I was in third grade and my dad scolded me for not saying thank you for a birthday present, which I'd quickly run off to play with because I loved it so much.

I would never tell my "friend" that she needed to work on something her son struggled with or question her approach. I counted on her for support, not judgment. Yes, Kelly was impulsive, unpredictable, and unresponsive to punishment, but we were trying on a lot of fronts.

Even if it didn't always seem like it, our situation had a lot of rare, positive elements wrapped up inside it as well. Kelly's outbursts and rebellions were actually strengths when it came to her being able to feel and express emotion. I was grateful she could stand up for herself, communicate, and share what she felt.

Even though we were a more confident unit and proud of our progress, Natalie was not wrong in what she said. Maybe it was completely true that Noah was easier, and responded more readily to discipline, but what good did it do to compare? Over and over I'd tell myself, when two things are uniquely different from one another, you just don't waste your time finding all the ways they don't align. They're different. Every child with autism is different. My child is uniquely herself.

We knew it was hard and would continue to be challenging, maybe for the rest of our lives. Fortunately, we had the awareness and energy to come at it from a different angle now—one we didn't even know existed four years prior.

Autism is complicated. That is all there is to it. Natalie, Scott, and I all saw and knew this, but we weren't going to let it hold us back as a family. Why? Because Kelly was working hard for herself, and she was working hard for us.

Above the front door of our house there's a large semi-circle window, which gives the front hall a warm, sunny glow most of the day. In the hallway by the front stairs, right outside her bedroom, was Kelly's favorite place to play with her Barbie dolls. In this sunny spot, she'd build elaborate Barbie scenes complete with mansions and convertibles, all dolls dressed to the nines in their glittery dresses, colorful high-heeled shoes, and pocketbooks.

Kelly spent endless hours designing and constructing weddings or fairytale balls, emulating scenes she'd watched over and over in Disney movies. Kelly was not really interested in "playing" house with her dolls. Instead, she wanted to build, design, and step back to see her finished product. Doing this calmed her and rejuvenated her confidence by showing her, with visual reinforcement, that she was really good at building and designing. She made sure every house had curtains, rugs, and matching furniture.

One time she asked Scott to make her an elevator for her homemade Barbie mansion. Happy to feed her creative side, he embraced the architectural challenge. With some string and cardboard, he fulfilled Kelly's wishes. Whenever she had a design flaw or obstacle, Scott came to her rescue with scissors, tape, string, paint, wood, or cardboard, whatever he could find to help her. They shared the same imaginative vision, and their teamwork was something they both appreciated and cherished.

The biggest changes in Kelly were yet to come. She was building them, making them happen, and I was carefully watching on the side, supporting her—her loyal, committed partner. Fear motivated me. Fear of her regressing to her worst days, going back to that unhappy, congested place. Above all, though, I continued to keep the faith, to chase hope, and to believe in Kelly. I had to keep the faith. It was the only way. Together, we'd keep building, one room at a time.

12

kelly's guardian angel

*"There is goodness and happiness in everything—you just
have to look for it."*

Dr. Patricia Kane came into our lives in the summer of 2005. On the
day of our first appointment, I was wearing jeans, a white t-shirt,
and comfortable shoes. Birkenstocks, I think. Kelly was dressed in
her favorite pair of pants, a soft cotton shirt, and sneakers. We'd
driven a little over an hour to get there, leaving Natalie at home with
Becca—a beloved babysitter she'd have fun with while Scott was
at work and we were gone. Anticipating a long morning, I packed
a snack for Kelly—a half dozen homemade almond butter truffles.

The waiting room was full of toys from games to puzzles, ani-
mals, dolls, cars, and trains. Clearly, many children had been there
before us. Along the wall was a white bookshelf with rows of open
square spaces that stacked magazines and books for parents or
adult patients. There were comfortable chairs to sit in with colorful squishy pillows. Kelly sat on the floor and played with the train
set and building blocks. She asked me to play with her while we
waited over an hour to see Dr. Kane. When the nurse finally led
us into Dr. Kane's office, Dr. Kane stood up from behind her desk
and walked over to meet us.

"Hi, Kelly." Dr. Kane calmly greeted her. "I'm so sorry to keep
you waiting." Dr. Kane bent over to gently touch Kelly's shoulder
while offering us an apology. Then she shook my hand and said,

"Nice to meet you both." The tone of her voice was soft but deliberate. It seemed each word was chosen carefully, giving the impression that she respected what we'd been through without even knowing the day-to-day grind or whole story yet. Kelly stared at a picture on the wall—a colorful sky at sunset with rocky mountains and a waterfall. The picture, plugged into the wall, was backlit and whispered the soft, soothing sound of the waterfall.

Dr. Kane shared Kelly's fascination: "Isn't that neat?"

While Kelly couldn't take her eyes off the picture, Dr. Kane's empathetic gaze focused on Kelly. It appeared almost as if she could see right through Kelly and knew what she needed without even having to dig deeper.

"Tell me what's going on with Kelly," Dr. Kane gently inquired while looking at both Kelly and me. Her compassionate grin showed interest in discovery, that there was no right or wrong answer. We reviewed Kelly's history together while Kelly sat on my lap. Dr. Kane was careful about what she said in front of Kelly so Kelly wouldn't feel frightened or upset by the details of what she heard. Rather, Dr. Kane wanted Kelly to understand the basics of what was going on in her body and how we were going to work toward helping her feel better.

Dr. Kane wasn't fazed by Kelly's behavior—how she fidgeted in the chair, flapped her hands, and clung to me, pulling my face toward hers when Dr. Kane asked me questions. Instead of judgment, Dr. Kane's mannerisms showed unwavering acceptance that spoke to her gentle, kindhearted way and desire to understand then treat the individual. In other words, Dr. Kane didn't jump right into "fixing" Kelly, which I liked.

During this first appointment, she talked to Kelly, not just to me, and connected with her on her level, which gained Kelly's trust. Although I did not know or understand it at the time, one of Dr. Kane's unique strengths was moving straight to the hearts of hurt children. She shared with me stories of other children she was working with, describing them as if they were little angels, gifts from God. Intuitively, I began to see how she adored them and made a deep connection with each child.

Having thirty years of experience under her belt, helping children with brain injuries, metabolic disorders, developmental delays, and autism, Dr. Kane, a nutritional biochemist PhD, asked a myriad of questions that no one had asked before. For example, instead of focusing on family or prenatal history, she was interested in knowing what our house was like, if Kelly had been exposed to any mold, lead paint, pesticides, or environmental toxins—things I'd never thought about.

Her training gave her the science background she needed to notice what was abnormal on a cellular level, and then her compassion kicked in, revealing her true talent: intuitively guiding the parent and child toward improving their health.

Dr. Kane had her own personal experiences in this area that she shared with me on that first visit. Her son had a stroke when he was only two years old. She'd spent many years traveling in the same shoes the parents of her patients walked in every day. Not only did she understand the challenge of dealing with sick children, she also knew how rewarding it was to find answers.

A month later, for the next appointment with Dr. Kane, I went alone. That meeting cleared the way for Kelly's treatment plan. Lab test results ordered by the medical doctor at the clinic where she worked, including a general chemistry panel and specialized fatty acid test from a university laboratory, determined the details of Dr. Kane's protocol for Kelly. When I walked in her office, Dr. Kane had all of Kelly's results neatly stacked in a pile in front of her, with yellow highlighted areas and notes made in red marker.

"We will start here, at the membrane level," Dr. Kane said, showing me a stunning image of the lipid membrane, the core of our being, something I'd never seen or thought about before. Her finger pointed to a diagram on an eight-by-ten-inch laminated card. The image was of purple-colored curly structures intricately swirled together and lined up in rows. The illustration was a microscopic view of the millions of membranes in our body.

Dr. Kane explained that at the membrane level, we could understand what went wrong and could then address it with specialized lipids called phospholipids. These would replace the ones that had been altered, causing Kelly's health complications.

"Kelly is working under a cloud of confusion due to hyperammonemia," Dr. Kane told me, referring to the evidence of Kelly's bloodwork. She pointed to Kelly's elevated BUN—blood urea nitrogen—score which indicated Kelly's liver was having trouble clearing excess ammonia. Then she elaborated, teaching me that when ammonia builds up due to impaired liver function, it can cause problems like confusion and seizures.

These clinical observations made a lot of intuitive sense to me based on how Kelly acted. Dr. Kane focused on Kelly's specific, individual features according to a variety of markers in her blood test results to decipher what might be happening and to determine how to help Kelly. With each irregularity, Dr. Kane had a specific explanation. For almost two hours, we talked about healing Kelly's body at its tiny core: the membrane level. Whenever I asked a question, she'd answer with examples that related directly to what was happening with Kelly. Even though I didn't understand everything she was talking about, this helped me trust her.

"It's all about the membrane," Dr. Kane reiterated, showing me more pictures of cellular structures, lipid membranes, and research papers. "The most important nutrient for the brain is fat, lipids. And not because the brain is made of 60 percent fat, but because of what specific fatty acids and phospholipids do for the brain." *No wonder my body craves fat*, I thought to myself. Knowing that information gave me another boost in confidence to listen to my body, to trust my instincts.

Dr. Kane's approach called for both oral and intravenous

therapy with phospholipids and balanced essential fatty acids. In the clinic where Dr. Kane worked, the medical doctor set up the oral and intravenous lipid regimes for Kelly.

"Intravenous, or IV, treatment is usually necessary to get the high doses needed for healing," Dr. Kane explained, specifying the reasons for IV therapy. "Large doses of phospholipids will not only reduce inflammation but also help heal or restore function in the cell membranes of Kelly's body. The IV treatment result is like scrubbing her DNA of any epigenetic insults and stabilizing her cell and organelle membranes."

The plan was for Kelly to get lipids through a push of nutrients directly into her blood. Since Kelly trusted Dr. Kane, she willingly agreed to the idea. Alongside the IV therapy, Kelly also had a list of supplements to take orally every day, some several times a day. I made a chart and checked them off as I gave them to her so I'd remember which ones, how much, and when I gave them to her.

Dr. Kane also suggested that we focus on "nutrient-dense" and organic foods for Kelly's diet—seeds, nuts, protein-rich foods, green veggies, berries, healthy fats, and oils. This was the Membrane Stabilizing Diet that Dr. Kane created years before and was very similar to what we were already doing on the SCD.

Between Kelly and Dr. Kane, there was a mutual understanding that few people had with Kelly. Dr. Kane understood her on a level that even I, her mother, was not able to. Dr. Kane quickly became my new mentor.

When one of the nurses complained about Kelly's behavior, saying she acted like a spoiled brat, Dr. Kane corrected her. She said to the nurse, "Kelly is ill, not spoiled. She is overwhelmed and frightened. Please be patient with her."

I'd never really thought about explaining it that way. Kelly was sick and that was what we were working on—healing her. The goal wasn't to fix her or solve autism. We just wanted to take away her pain, plain and simple, and yet complex at the same time.

"Just being there, truly connected with someone who is ill, is so important." Dr. Kane encouraged me to focus on caring for Kelly in a gentle, devoted manner. I needed to hear this since I was still searching for answers, trying to make sense of the ongoing challenges.

Even though Kelly was on the SCD and making progress, she continued to need the antifungal medication, Lamisil. It was a crutch we couldn't get rid of. Every time we tried, it was a nightmare with sleepless nights and regressive negative behaviors, anger, and rage. That was one of the reasons I went to Dr. Kane—to get Kelly off prescription antifungal medications and to explore any other means of addressing the underlying issue.

When I asked Dr. Kane about the Lamisil, she reassured me, "Don't worry, we'll get to that."

Then, Dr. Kane gave me the most important advice I'd received from anyone. I'd heard it before, and believed it to be true, but this time it sunk in much deeper.

"Tell her you love her no matter what, Suzie," Dr. Kane counseled me, pausing as if remembering a similar time in her own life. "Reassure her and always acknowledge her feelings."

Her guidance offered enlightenment and acceptance that lifted a huge weight off my shoulders. Dr. Kane's words validated my instinct to be by Kelly's side, loving her first and foremost. She reminded me that communicating with love and constant encouragement would keep us on the right path. That encouragement to let go of expectations and missed milestones had been missing. Pressure to do otherwise came from external sources like Kelly's therapists, teachers, friends, and family members. I needed to reassure her with my love. It was so simple, so beautiful.

A few weeks later, on the day of Kelly's first IV treatment, Kelly flapped her hands in front of her face as we walked into Dr. Kane's office. She was grumpy, hyper, distant, and distracted. I was a bit nervous, having never done anything like this before, and harboring my own phobia of needles. Luckily, Kelly was oblivious. The nurse put numbing cream on Kelly's arm which took about thirty minutes to work.

When it was time, Kelly sat perfectly still while the nurse pushed the nutrients into her arm intravenously. Fifteen minutes later, Kelly was a totally different child.

She looked right at me, smiled, and calmly asked, "Mom, can I go to the bathroom?"

She'd never asked me that in her life. Shocked by the immediate change in her mood, language, processing, and compliance, I wanted to shout a victorious cheer, jump up and down, and then hug Dr. Kane.

Within a few months, after maybe a dozen of these fast IV push treatments, several consultations, and more bloodwork, Kelly transitioned to longer treatments that dripped intravenously over three hours. Before giving Kelly anything, Dr. Kane always tried it on herself first. She shared this with Kelly: "I just did it on myself and it worked really, really well. You just sit in a super comfy chair and watch whatever movies you want while the IV drips into your arm. Mom will be with you the whole time."

When she spoke to Kelly, it was as if they were partners, equals. Then, Dr. Kane turned her gaze to me and reiterated, "Really, I don't do IV therapy on anyone before testing it on myself." That boosted her credibility even further in my mind.

The numbing cream was a necessity. It worked like magic. Kelly didn't feel a thing. The nurse instructed Kelly to sit as still as possible, and, to my amazement, Kelly complied. It was like she knew and accepted what she needed to do because she could feel the benefits. Kelly wanted the IV.

Movies always entranced Kelly. During her three hours of IV therapy, Kelly sat in a leather recliner with her feet up and her arm propped up by squishy pillows so she could hold it perfectly straight and still. With a cozy fuzzy blanket draped over her, she watched movies on a compact DVD player. I sat next to her, keeping an eye on her the entire time, and hopped up to get drinks or snacks whenever she needed something. We were surrounded by other patients getting similar treatments for Lyme, multiple sclerosis, fibromyalgia, chronic fatigue syndrome, poststroke, brain injury, Parkinson's, seizures, and other chronic illnesses.

Dr. Kane and the clinic medical director monitored Kelly's bloodwork and progress, which we reviewed in consultations every few months. After several months of IV treatments following Dr. Kane's protocol, the PK Protocol, Kelly's BUN normalized. The same was true of her low white blood count, elevated liver enzymes, and other markers that had been out of range. Eventually, we were also able to successfully ween Kelly off the Lamisil without any adverse side effects. It was a miracle.

Kelly blossomed. The allergic shiners, the puffy dark circles under her eyes, faded after each IV treatment. The pinkish hue in her cheeks returned, and her bowels normalized. She had more expression in her face, she was less frustrated with daily tasks or chores, she even started to describe her feelings, wants, and needs more clearly, vividly in fact.

Kelly's response time and engagement in conversation showed she could also better grasp what was being said around her. She processed information and situations much faster. I could understand her better, too. These were almost immediate and very distinct responses, directly correlated to the IV treatments. Without a doubt, I was convinced we were finally witnessing undeniable, legitimate healing in Kelly, as Dr. Kane had so elaborately illustrated, at the membrane level.

By December of 2006, Kelly was in her third year at the Janus School. For the first two years, she was in a classroom with only three other students, all on the high-functioning end of the autism spectrum. This year, they moved Kelly to a new classroom with eight other students and a different teacher. The curriculum was at a fourth-grade level and the teacher used textbooks—a completely different model than the classroom Kelly had been in the previous two years. Kelly was overwhelmed, lost, and couldn't follow along. It was reminiscent of her first-grade experience. Scott and I agreed we needed to get some outside professional advice about whether or not Janus would continue to be the right fit, and if not, potentially explore other options.

We went back to Dr. Mary Keith, a well-respected, independent school psychologist in Lititz, Pennsylvania, thirty miles from our house. Dr. Keith had done educational and psychological testing on Kelly back in 2004 when Kelly had been in first grade and the public school hadn't been meeting her needs. One of the outcomes of that evaluation was that Dr. Keith had recommended Lindamood-Bell to teach Kelly foundational reading skills, which ended up being remarkably beneficial.

This time, Dr. Keith did a similar battery of tests including the WISC-IV test of intelligence, the TONI-3 (test of nonverbal intelligence), TOPL (test of pragmatic language), and about ten others. The testing was done over a period of several weeks in two separate, two-hour long appointments. The end result was a forty-page report detailing test scores and recommended accommodations or placements based on specific aspects of Kelly's functioning. Dr. Keith was very thorough in documenting her observations as if every detail was some sort of clue. In her report, she wrote the following:

Kelly was evaluated on two separate days, one week apart. On the first day of testing on November 29, 2006, Kelly was a bit reluctant to accompany the examiner into the testing room and became distracted with internal thoughts. She had a stuffed animal with her and was very clingy to her toy, not wanting to part from it. She was methodical in completing testing tasks and appeared to want to do well but needed frequent breaks to maintain attention and concentration.

On the day before Kelly's second testing appointment with Dr. Keith, Kelly had an IV treatment. When Kelly was tested after her IV, the psychologist noticed the dramatic change in Kelly's mood, focus, and processing. She continued the dialogue in her report documenting this remarkable shift:

> *Kelly had an intravenous lipid treatment on the day before her second day of testing on December 7, 2006, which had an observably favorable impact on her. Kelly was chatty and smiled, separated from her mother with no difficulty, engaged in the give-and-take of verbal conversation, and was very hard working on all testing tasks. She had an American Girl doll with her which she brought into the testing room but was not at all distracted by the toy and remained very hard working and focused and cooperative during the session.*

> *Although Kelly was cooperative on both testing dates, she was clearly better able to maintain engagement, attention, focus, and concentration throughout the second evaluation following her treatment. She also appeared to be brighter and more alert.*

After thoroughly reviewing Dr. Keith's evaluation report, Scott and I met with her to discuss her feedback. We were immensely disappointed to learn that Dr. Keith's findings revealed that Kelly had not made any documented educational progress since her last testing two years prior. That, coupled with Kelly's recent school frustrations, helped us to decide we needed a new school placement for Kelly. Janus was no longer a good fit for her.

Scott and I requested a special education placement meeting with our public school district. As parents, we wanted a nurturing learning environment molded to Kelly's particular level based on test scores, not appearances, and one that also respected her social and emotional needs. We didn't expect the best or anything out of the ordinary—just something that offered the appropriate adaptations with instructors who'd been trained on how to handle autism.

During our IEP meeting with the school district, the special education director recommended placing Kelly in a fifth-grade mainstream classroom with twenty or so other students. Wait, I thought, *that goes against everything that Dr. Keith documented in her report!*

My lips parted then my jaw dropped in shock at this preposterous idea. I wanted to scream but somewhere, I don't know where, I found the composure to clamp my mouth shut and clench my teeth together. In a continued effort to keep from lashing out, I crossed my arms tightly across my chest, pushing my fingertips into my ribs.

Then I looked at the fifth-grade teacher, Mrs. Jones, sitting diagonally across the table from me. Mrs. Jones and I had a connection since she had been one of Natalie's teachers. She, too, looked surprised.

I took a deep breath in and out through my nose. Feeling slightly more composed and hoping to tackle this through a back door approach, I asked Mrs. Jones, "Do you use textbooks to teach the classroom materials, and are they at a fifth-grade reading and comprehension level?"

"Yes." She shrugged and ever so slightly shook her head in disagreement with the special education director.

Exasperated, I continued: "And students are expected to follow along?"

Mrs. Jones nodded and replied, "Yes. And we move quickly through the materials." Her eyes lingered on mine, giving me a look of agreement that this was not an appropriate fit for Kelly.

This was clearly not an option based on Dr. Keith's findings. If Kelly's reading comprehension tested at a first-grade level, she wouldn't be able to work with fifth-grade textbooks. And if her processing speed was less than the .1 percentile, meaning she processed slower than 99.9 percent of all children her age, there was no way she could sit in a classroom of twenty fifth-graders and follow the teacher. *What are they thinking? How dare they put Kelly in that position!* Anger boiled in my belly while my pulse rapidly picked up speed, reverberating throughout my chest.

The special education director had the reputation of being a bully. Her big brother approach engaged fear tactics and used a condescending style with parents, which naturally was not child driven. In fact, she blatantly ignored the individual student's specific needs and test scores, expecting the student to fit the school's already existing program.

Scott and I agreed that Kelly would be even more miserable at our home school district than at Janus. For Kelly's sake, we were determined not to repeat mistakes we'd already learned from.

Instead, we chose to rely on experts we could trust. With school decisions, Dr. Keith advised us. She understood we were in a pickle given our limited choices based on location and need, but adamantly clarified that homeschooling or cyber-school were definitely not alternatives. I agreed. Kelly was extremely attached to me, and since focusing was an issue for her, being at home would be way too distracting.

Searching desperately for options, we even considered Catholic schools in the area despite the fact that we weren't Catholic. Then suddenly, it hit me. Out of the blue, I remembered that the Montessori school Kelly had attended for preschool and kindergarten had opened an elementary school that went up to eighth grade. I asked Dr. Keith about it, and with the proper modifications, she thought it could work.

Eager about the possibility, I immediately called Montessori and spoke with Cindy, the director who'd recommended we get Kelly help back when she was still in preschool.

"It's so nice to hear from you!" Cindy said, welcoming my call.

"How are Natalie and Kelly?" She hadn't seen them since they were in kindergarten, five and seven years earlier. I filled her in, leading to my purpose for calling. We scheduled a meeting for the next day.

Wanting to honor Kelly's specific needs, I brought the report from Dr. Keith. After reviewing the key points, Cindy was confident it would work, that Kelly could come back. After all, she reminded me, Montessori's approach was multidimensional and they encouraged self-paced learning. Then Cindy shared with me that there were already two children with autism in the classroom of eight elementary students. Kelly would become the third.

"They are like family to each other," Cindy said, describing the small group that had been together in the same classroom for years. The following day, I picked Kelly up early from Janus and took her to visit Montessori. Given the addition of the elementary classroom and growing student body, the school had moved to a new location since Kelly attended preschool and kindergarten.

With a warm welcome from the elementary students and smiling familiar faces from the past like Maria's, Kelly was excited to go back. She started right after Christmas break in January of 2007.

A few months later, Kelly was acclimated back into Montessori, had made a few friends, and liked her new routine. One night before dinner, and a few days after an IV treatment, I asked Kelly if she remembered she had homework. Though she had accepted it was a necessary evil and was trying to get used to it, Kelly hated homework and put it off as long as possible. On this particular night, her response to my prodding shocked me.

Instead of a protest, she calmly and politely said, "Yeah, Mom, that's why I came downstairs. And for dinner too. Can I have dinner first, then do my homework?"

For about thirty days after her IV treatments, Kelly was exceedingly compliant, quick to process, and eager to talk. It continued to blow my mind. I was conversing with my daughter in a way that I'd dreamt about before but assumed might never happen.

We were speaking to one another instead of at one another. We were expressing ourselves, asking questions, hearing one another. Conversations like this never happened before the IV treatments.

I continued, hoping to keep the momentum: "Sorry, Kelly, dinner's not ready yet. How about if you do your homework first, okay?"

"Sure," Kelly said, sitting down at the kitchen table and starting her homework on her own without a single complaint.

"Oops, I dropped a scrap of paper on the floor. I'll get it," Kelly confidently and calmly declared. Before, just months ago, that scenario would have ignited a major tantrum.

As she worked at the kitchen table with her pencil and paper, Kelly continued her happy, polite articulations: "Mom, I'm hungry. When will dinner be ready?"

"It's almost ready, Kelly," I lovingly replied, sprinkling a little salt and pepper on the stir fry.

"Whatcha making, Mom?" she asked, observing me without her usual confusion or anger over my serious expression of concentration while cooking.

"Steak with some green beans. Sound good?" I hoped her cheerful mood would continue.

"Sounds great, Mom," Kelly said, continuing her homework at the table. "Rats! I dropped another paper on the floor." She giggled and then moved on, intently finishing her homework. This was the miracle we'd been waiting for. Finally.

Up until this point, I'd been confidently navigating a healthy lifestyle on my own, following the SCD, eating all the "right" foods, and taking supplements that seemed helpful like fish oil, probiotics, calcium, and magnesium. Then, at age forty-two, my eczema resurfaced, my libido plummeted, flatulence became a regular post-meal occurrence, and I started having heart palpitations. It was my turn, I told myself. I decided to consult with Dr. Kane to get her advice on targeted supplementation and diet based on my bloodwork, just like we'd done with Kelly.

The results were illuminating. My body craved the same phospholipids that Kelly needed, not fish oil. Food testing showed eggs and a handful of other foods I hadn't suspected, like kale, were triggers for me. Dr. Kane recommended adding some enzymes to help me digest certain foods more effectively without flatulence or bloating. We also added in some other supplements my body was asking for like evening primrose oil and CoQ10.

It was a huge step for me to seek out help and invest in my own health, not just Kelly's. Having Dr. Kane's guidance was a priceless gift I gave myself. There was no doubt in my mind she was the hero we'd been looking for and Kelly's guardian angel.

One day, while driving home after our monthly visit to Dr. Kane's office, Kelly pressed her forehead against the car window to look up into the sky. Something up there fascinated her and she crooked her neck to capture a good look at it. Her eyes fixed on whatever it was while her mouth opened in a pleasant smile as if someone was whispering happy thoughts to her.

"Mom, I see angels, beautiful angels," Kelly said, beaming and still staring up at the sky. I assumed she meant clouds in the shape of angels.

"That's so cool, Kelly!" After a short pause, just to be sure, I clarified: "Do you mean clouds that look like angels?"

Still staring out the window and smiling, she insisted, "No, Mom. I really see angels, their wings and beautiful faces."

Back in the beginning of our journey, people used to tell me, in some attempt to comfort, that God only gives you what you can handle. I wanted to lash out, tell them off, take out all my frustration out on that false, highly flawed cliché. At the time, I thought there was no way God would impose autism on my daughter, on our family. It felt more like a random punishment than a predetermined destiny.

After years of cleaning up my diet and being Kelly's partner, my perspective and thoughts had dramatically changed. Now I had a glimpse of the deeper purpose in all of this. Kelly was my greatest teacher, and that was part of a bigger plan. I started to believe that, even if I didn't know every step of that plan.

Everything had shifted. The darkness was now becoming light. The clouds parted. Kelly could see angels around us. I had to believe her even though I didn't see them myself.

13

lessons from joshua

"It's truly the best feeling ever when you get really swept away while doing something."

"Suzie, did you ever think about being a nurse?" my dad asked me, humbled by his intense pain and the stiff cotton hospital gown that draped his naked skinny body.

His lips parted in an effort to smile before praising me: "Because I think you'd make a really good one." He relished the gentle way I adjusted the pillow behind his head to minimize the pain in his neck while he lay in the hospital bed, barely able to move.

I hesitated before answering as I considered the possibility. The way he'd softened and surrendered to my care made me appreciate the time alone with him, even if it wasn't under the best of circumstances. The corners of my lips turned upward, wrinkling my cheeks and eyes before I spoke.

"No, I never did. I didn't think I could handle the blood and needles." Then, thinking about it a little more, I realized after all I'd been through with Kelly, I probably could.

His yellowed teeth emerged in a pained but loving expression so he could share a rare compliment: "You're the most patient person in the world." Then he closed his eyes and drifted off to sleep.

My dad was at Mass General Hospital being treated for myelodysplastic syndrome, or MDS. That was the end of April 2012, three years after I'd become a health coach.

There were only a few times I could remember when I imagined working or, more likely, volunteering in a hospital. One was when I was a teenager and I really wanted to be a candy striper—a hospital volunteer job that got its name from the light pink and white striped uniform. The second was in 1991 when I was a newly married career woman working in the world of finance. Every evening on my way home from work, I drove past a hospital. Inevitably, I'd glance over at it and think that I should be in there, helping. I'd wonder what I could do to be of service. It was a strange instinct, considering I was educated and working in business and never had a proclivity for medicine. Two fleeting examples of times that entering health care came to mind, but they never materialized.

Wherever that urge came from, it resurfaced again in 2008. With almost four years being Kelly's partner on the SCD and continuing to work closely with Dr. Kane, I had a deep desire to learn about nutrition and biochemistry. It was transforming our lives, which sparked a serious longing to know more and use that knowledge to help others. *Maybe this is my destiny after all?*

After doing some research online, the program that seemed to fit best with my life and family was Integrative Nutrition. It was a little less than a year-long study with classes in New York City on weekends. The course would be like dipping my toe in the water—not a huge commitment of either time or money.

Scott was extremely supportive of my desire to learn more. He admired my determination and all the progress I'd been able to facilitate for Kelly. My sisters, my fitness trainer, my therapist, and the few friends who I told I was thinking about the program consistently encouraged me.

"You can help so many people," they said.

Yet, I grappled with the decision, feeling like I couldn't possibly do this for me. The trouble was leaving Kelly for all the weekends I'd be in class. She was still so dependent on me. I was her chef, best friend, companion, round-the-clock therapist, and caregiver. Simply put, I was her soft, cuddly Linus blankie. My worst fear was that she would regress if I left her; that I would lose her. Guilt and indecision plagued me.

The turning point in my decision came when I sat on the couch next to my friend Maggie, who I'd known since I was nine years old. My oldest sister's best friend since fifth grade, Maggie was like another big sister. It was a cold, dreary day in early November. A hot mug of tea warmed the palm of my hands as I revealed my dilemma and solicited Maggie's advice.

"You have to do it," Maggie declared, staring at me with conviction while leaning in closer and placing one hand on my knee. Her encouragement bubbled effortlessly from a place of love, support, and respect. The way in which she so easily made the decision for me told me that no matter what the outcome, it would be good for me. Tears dribbled down my cheeks at the thought of doing something for myself and then using that knowledge to help others.

"Look what you've done with Kelly. It's incredible," Maggie praised me, her own tears pooling in the corners of her eyes. "Now you can help other people with not only your personal experience but expertise."

I knew how far we'd come, but hadn't really paused to look behind me and appreciate the distance or magnitude of it all. My arms reached out and hugged her.

Helping people was what I longed for—connection to others and expanding the love beyond my family. It had been so long since I'd been able to even think about giving to anyone else because I couldn't see beyond what was right in front of me. In that moment, it was done. I'd made my decision.

Two months later, in January of 2009, classes began at Integrative Nutrition in New York City. The program was transformational on many levels. First, it got me away from Kelly, which we both needed. In my absence, she learned to count on her dad in a new way. The separation also gave me the necessary space to start exploring a passion beyond healing her or myself.

The timing was perfect. At this point in her treatment with Dr. Kane, Kelly was much more compliant and had better comprehension of language and situations around her. Thankfully, she understood why I was leaving, where I was going, and when I'd be back.

I'd wake up early Saturday morning, shower, and then drive into Manhattan. Without traffic, it only took a little over two hours. By eight o'clock, I was in my designated parking garage on West End Avenue. When class was over at five o'clock in the afternoon, I'd drive out of the city to spend the night with my sister and her family in New Jersey. The next morning, I'd commute back into New York. At the end of Sunday's classes, I got in my car and headed home, arriving back around eight o'clock in the evening.

During our lunch breaks, I did something I hadn't done since the girls were born—get out, alone, and wander without a plan, seeing where my feet would take me. Walking the streets around Lincoln Center set the stage for a sense of freedom and exploration I'd been missing for a long time.

On the very first day of class, I walked by myself down to Columbus Circle for lunch at Whole Foods. I made a salad and sat down at one of the only open seats, which happened to be next to two women who looked like they were also Integrative Nutrition students. I introduced myself, and we all shared how we'd decided to register in the program. They'd come to New York from Ohio.

Like me, they were moms who wanted to expand their healthy eating values beyond their family. One of them, Carrie, had a bubbly, happy demeanor that reminded me of a cheerleader. She'd had a transformational experience being coached by a graduate of Integrative Nutrition, which inspired her to enroll. When I started to tell them the story of Kelly, how our journey sparked my interest in learning about nutrition, they listened intently as if I was sharing breaking news that hadn't been broadcast yet.

"I could listen to you talk all day," Carrie said, beaming at me and gushing with a yearning to hear more. For the first time, I had an audience who, surprisingly, was curious about the path I'd been pioneering.

The Integrative Nutrition curriculum was multidimensional. It taught a variety of dietary theories along with coaching skills. In the process, it also challenged us to dig deeper into our own sense of self.

Joshua Rosenthal, the founder of Integrative Nutrition, led the program with his soothing, strong voice and magnetic presence. Around his tall, slim body and bald head, there was an almost angelic aura that radiated outward, setting the tone for healing through loving guidance. Sitting there amongst my fellow students, passionate men and women eager to change the pace of health in our world, I felt part of a new tribe.

Several times a day during class, Joshua walked up and down the aisles with a microphone, encouraging students to share stories, ask questions, or give their own perspective on topics. With over a thousand students, it wasn't easy to get picked. A few times, our eyes met, but I never got a chance at the microphone.

Waiting in line to go into class one Saturday morning, I struck up a conversation with a woman from Florida. She had a son with disabilities who'd been in a wheelchair for years. With so much to share about the neverending responsibility of parenting children with special needs, we became buddies and sat with each other every class after that. There were many other students I'd connected with, including a nutritionist from California, a doctor from Canada, a psychologist from Florida, and another mom with a son on the autistic spectrum from Vermont.

In addition to live classes, there were online learning modules with teachers from all types of holistic healing modalities. Joshua also recorded coaching sessions that modeled his method of creating a safe space for clients to share. I listened to Joshua's coaching sessions over and over again, training myself to be the best possible coach.

I began to understand and believe that the coaching wasn't about teaching nutrition or lifestyle adjustments as much as it was about empowerment. The idea was that we wouldn't tell clients what to do until we fully understood their pain points, needs, and desires. The client would lead the way, and we would meet them there, guiding and supporting them in the process.

The course had a few requirements like passing several tests and completing a series of practice coaching sessions with other students. With almost everyone I met during class, I'd ask if they'd like to role-play what was called a health history session—what would become an initial consultation with a client. We'd do this over the phone once we were all back in our own homes. I enjoyed these sessions so much that I spent hours with other students, pretending to walk them through an initial consultation and allowing them to do the same with me. These practice coaching sessions challenged me to ask open-ended questions instead of questions with a yes or no answer. It changed the way I communicated with everyone—Natalie, Kelly, Scott, my extended family, and friends.

Over the years, in conversation with Kelly, I'd learned to choose my words carefully, keeping them simple and to the point, often not talking much to avoid frustrating her. Now, with the freedom to explore this new arsenal of skills, I'd found my voice again. I tried to open up more conversation and connection with others by using probing questions.

Natalie and Scott were my guinea pigs. I practiced on them daily. It became a game in my head where I'd craft questions that would hopefully spark a conversation, set me up for listening, and set them up for talking. Questions like "So, what's one thing that went well today?" or "What are you excited about at school right now?" instead of a simple "How was your day?" I wanted to know not just what happened, but how they felt about it. Communication and conversation were things I'd always valued and craved, and I was excited to bring them back into my life in a meaningful way.

In one of the over a thousand seats in the theater at Lincoln Center, I sat with a notebook on my lap and pen in hand. During every Integrative Nutrition class, I wrote pages of notes, soaking up every possible nugget of enlightenment and learning. When Dr. Jonathan Rechtschaffen, cofounder of the Omega Institute, spoke about food intolerances, my legs started jittering. I couldn't sit still. It was our story. I wanted to jump up and shout, "Yes, it's true!" Kelly and I were among many who'd been healed by removing food triggers. This was the confirmation I needed that this theory went beyond autism.

On the day Dr. Mark Hyman stood on stage to teach us, it felt like a rock star entered the room. And that smile. His smile charmed us all. One of his first PowerPoint slides was a picture of himself, sick with dark circles under his eyes, like mine and Kelly's. He shared his story of chronic fatigue syndrome and how he healed it with diet and functional medicine—an exploration of underlying causes of symptoms or disease and how various bodily functions are connected.

The next slide he showed was a photograph of Dr. Sid Baker. Shocked and excited, I wanted to raise my hand, stand up, and shout, *I know him! He was my daughter's doctor!* Dr. Hyman referred to Dr. Baker as the founder of functional medicine. I got goosebumps thinking about it. Everything Mark Hyman said in his presentation was exactly what we had learned through our experience with Dr. Baker. More and more people were embracing what we had been doing with our dietary changes. Finally, we were no longer on an island.

Other greats were Geneen Roth and Victoria Moran, who shared their own personal journeys of emotional eating and wisdom around reframing food to boost self-esteem. A nutritionist taught us about the science of digestion. Marion Nestle, Annmarie Colbin, and Paul Pitchford spoke of the importance of clean whole food. Watching Dr. Andrew Weil do a breathing meditation on stage, directly in front of me, invited and inspired the holistic healing approach of thinking beyond food.

Julia Cameron, who wrote *The Artist's Way*, sang to us after sharing how she'd always been teased by her musical family that she couldn't sing. Julia taught us something she invented called "morning pages," which was three pages of longhand stream of consciousness writing done upon waking in the morning. The importance of this exercise wasn't just to spew thoughts or purge feelings. Julia explained how it would connect you to your deeper self. The next morning, I woke up thirty minutes earlier so I could write my first set of morning pages before driving back into New York City for another day of classes.

With seven months of in-person and online learning, we acquired a vast knowledge of a wide variety of different dietary theories, but we also learned a lot about ourselves. There were some things I didn't fully agree with like the approach of adding in more whole grains since I'd greatly benefited from a grain-free diet. Though I did fully subscribe to the idea of making vegetables the main course.

Quinoa and kale were two big buzz words. During class one Saturday, I was introduced to kale for the first time. Joshua stood on stage, in a white apron and tall chef's hat, showing us how to remove the kale leaves from the stalks by simply holding the stem with one hand and pulling down the leaves with the other hand, stripping the leaves off the stem.

Joshua introduced his own brilliant philosophies like bio-individuality. Bio-individuality is the concept that there is no one perfect way of eating that works for everybody. While science and medicine preached standard dietary approaches or a magic bullet that will work for all Americans, Joshua challenged that theory.

Live, during classes, and in his recordings, Joshua taught us to treat each individual, including ourselves, as singularly precious. His belief was that each and every person has their own constitution of unique needs based on heredity, blood type, health, lifestyle, age, and gender. I'd add digestion to that list. For example, someone with irritable bowel syndrome might not be able to eat raw vegetables or flax seeds. In other words, what had worked for me, may not work for someone else. In approaching clients using Joshua's theory of bio-individuality, we, as health coaches, would connect with them on a much deeper level to find out what they really needed without forcing them to eat kale and quinoa just because those foods are healthy choices.

During one lecture, Joshua introduced another concept that would surprisingly tame his students' passion around a healthy diet. That theory was orthorexia. Orthorexia is an unhealthy obsession with healthy food. With my enduring healthy eating habits and strict adherence to the SCD, I started to contemplate whether or not I was orthorexic.

For several years, I'd been so concerned, neurotic even, you could say, about controlling our diet, worrying about every crumb that entered our bodies, cooking around the clock and consistently ordering plain food anytime I traveled or ate out. At the end of Joshua's segment on orthorexia, I raised my hand, hoping to be called on, but wasn't.

I was never diagnosed with orthorexia or any other eating disorder, but there were times in my past, in the tense, rigid days of the SCD, where I may have fit that profile.

Without intending to, Scott reminded me of this possibility once while we were enjoying a relaxing evening out on our deck after dinner. We weren't talking about eating habits or diet at all, but that's where we ended up.

It started with me nervously saying to him, "I have something I want to tell you. A confession of sorts."

He folded his arms across his chest and gave me a quizzical, apprehensive look, hesitating to reply: "Okay."

"My left breast is larger than my right," I said, and then paused, took a breath, and swallowed. There, I'd said it. I didn't think he observed this difference, which had only become more pronounced in the past few months.

"It's really noticeable when I wear a bathing suit. One side of the bikini top is too small and the other too big. It's also visible when I wear tighter shirts or bend over in front of a mirror, like when I'm working out at the gym."

I paused again, gearing up for the real point: "I'm feeling really self-conscious about it and just wanted you to know. While I'm not planning to do anything to correct it, I wonder if anyone else notices, if I should be embarrassed."

"Oh, that doesn't bother me, Suzie." His eyes softened and locked with mine in a convincingly adoring way.

"I love your body. All of it," he blurted out in relief of my seemingly silly admission. He loved me, crooked or not. What I saw as blemishes, he saw as perfect imperfections.

"Honestly, it bothers me more that you eat the way you do. I mean that we can't go out to eat, and you have to cook all the time."

It seemed like an out-of-the-blue admission, but I knew he was right. Most of the time, I was a slave to the kitchen, cooking everything we ate from scratch. His comment made me examine my eating habits from a different perspective, his perspective: was I too rigid, too narrow minded, too stressed about food? Were we missing out on fun because of the way I ate?

I liked being authentically loyal to my ways, but hearing Scott's viewpoint and being reminded of Joshua's lecture, I was inspired to relax a bit.

No, I wasn't orthorexic. Thankfully, there were inherent reasons why I didn't obsess to the point of being unhealthy. For one,

Integrative Nutrition was showing me how to keep a fixed loyalty to my specific health motives and routine while also honoring my body in an almost spiritual fashion, honoring it as a temple. In being rigid, I was merely following the SCD with an intent to heal and honor my body. As validation and positive reinforcement, I reminded myself of that loving intention.

Yet, I knew that I needed to be flexible within my strength—not by indulging in the wrong things, but in how I perceived and prepared our food. Joshua taught me to invite more freedom and love into my cooking. I didn't tell my family anything had changed with how I'd be making dinner, but inside, it felt so good to think of how I was caring for them with my cooking. Cooking became a form of pampering for all of us instead of an exhausting chore I'd endure alone.

Looking back to November, when I enrolled in Integrative Nutrition, I didn't fully understand what I'd do afterwards. But a few months into the program, I became passionate about wanting to coach others on diet and lifestyle, specifically digestion. The experience I'd had with my own healing and Kelly's, coupled with lesson tools from classes, made me feel confident and ready.

Clients came to me with irritable bowel, constipation, or belly aches that we'd view from many angles, ruling out food triggers among other possibilities while we worked together. Transformation and healing excited me. There was no greater reward than seeing someone's life change dramatically for the better. This was the most gratifying job I'd ever done. By the time I graduated in July 2009, I had twenty paying clients that I'd gotten exclusively through word of mouth, and I wanted more.

When I started coaching, my dad gave me his office. This was a huge vote of confidence, a reward, considering all the years he doubted my health challenges and thought I overcompensated for Kelly's diet. Now, I believed he saw value in me and my new career. It was a large corner office with two big windows in the building where Bachman corporate personnel worked, including Scott, president of the company.

On one side of my dad's office was a large dark wood bookcase, littered with dusty race car paraphernalia and old photographs. I packed them in a box and replaced them with my diet and health books. On the walls, I hung my certificates along with pictures that spoke of relaxation and healthy living. Scott's office was two doors down from mine. Scott loved having me there during the day so we could have conversations that never seemed to happen at night when he got home.

One of the biggest lessons Kelly learned was to listen to her body and connect the dots between what she ate and how she felt, which became a key part of the work I was doing with my clients. We'd sit down together and, piece by piece, identify their individual food triggers—still a new concept for most. The results, in terms of general everyday well-being, alertness, and clarity, were mind-blowing. Weight loss was also a repeated and unexpected benefit from clients removing food triggers and following my clean eating plan.

Sitting across from my client, I wanted to make sure she felt safe and free to share as much or as little as she wanted. After a couple of meetings, I could tell that she did. Listening with love, acceptance, and absence of judgment, I tried to create this for her.

"Walk me through your day," I'd ask her.

She'd skip breakfast because she wasn't hungry. Then, around eleven in the morning, she'd grab a power bar on the go. Lunch was usually another wrapped goodie or nothing at all. So, by four o'clock in the afternoon, she'd be ravenous and start craving a glass of wine. Her body was hungry for nourishment and pause.

"Would you consider stopping and having lunch?" I gently inquired, hoping to show I appreciated the challenge. I didn't want to lecture her on how breakfast was the most important meal of the day. She didn't need that. Instead, I said, "I think your body could use some real food. What do you think?"

"Yes," she said, surrendering to the idea, knowing it was about the self-care she longed for but had been denying herself. Intuitively, she knew what she needed: "I can do that."

"How about a salad with hardboiled eggs and chicken, or leftovers from dinner?" I suggested a few ideas and continued with a vision for her: "See if you can slow down and chew your food, savoring every bite as if eating is pampering yourself. Maybe plan lunch out with a friend."

By simply taking time for herself to sit with me, talk about her lifestyle, and brainstorm ideas, she was engaging in a journey of self-love that fed off itself. At first, it was awkward for her and felt selfish, but I encouraged her to do it anyway. She needed reminding that she was worth it. At the end of her almost hour-long sessions, she'd thank me for the ideas and breakthroughs. One day, I leaned closer to her as if to hug her, but didn't.

Instead, I shared my intrinsic reward with her: "You know, one of the greatest things about being a health coach is the ability to share an inherent desire to accept and love others."

Shortly after I started seeing a steady, healthy cycle of clients, Natalie and I were at Ulta shopping for perfume and makeup when we ran into a client of mine, Sally.

"You know, your mom saved my life," Sally told Natalie. Natalie looked at me with a slight grin that conveyed unspoken understanding and pride. Once Natalie and I were done shopping and back in the car, I shared Sally's radical story of transformation and healing. I wasn't sure Natalie wanted to hear all the details but decided to tell her anyway.

I began by briefly divulging Sally's history. I told Natalie that when Sally first came to see me, she was suffering from horrible stomach pains and acid reflux. It was so bad that she had to cut back her physical activity. Her husband wanted her to go see a specialist at Jefferson Hospital in Philadelphia, but she told him she wanted to try dietary changes first and was referred to me.

I let Natalie in on how Sally, instead of tackling an elimination diet, preferred to do food sensitivity testing. This was something I was able to do for my clients through a lab in Florida. Sally's test showed she had a severe reaction to wheat and moderate sensitivities to other foods including dairy. Once she changed her diet, eliminating those food triggers, the transformation was mind-blowing—her stomach pains went away and her energy soared.

Natalie was listening and seemed interested, so I kept going. "Sally works long hours and travels frequently for her job, so eating according to plan was a challenge for her. Step-by-step guidance was really the ticket to her success." I revealed to Natalie what it meant for me to be a support system for Sally. I shared the honor and excitement I felt from standing by Sally and watching her achieve her goals, how she accepted a new lifestyle and then pushed herself to hold on to it.

"What Sally really meant when she said I saved her life, Natalie, was that changing her eating habits gave her back her life," I said, pausing, "her freedom, her energy, her health. She could finally feel like herself again. How cool is that?"

Natalie was smiling, her sharp intuition calculating my personal investment in my new career path. "That's amazing, Mom, really amazing."

After a brief silence, I thanked Natalie for listening. Then, with the way she gazed out the car window, I could tell she was done. Like with many topics, Natalie didn't need to engage in long conversations; that wasn't her style. She didn't have to tell me she was proud of my work. I was content, beaming really, to know she'd heard it from someone else. For several years, I'd felt Kelly's pride and gratitude; that day, I got to feel it from Natalie, too. It meant more to me than I ever could have imagined. Knowing she'd listened, and was proud, was enough for me, too.

A few months later during Natalie's senior year of high school, she came into the kitchen while I was preparing lunch. I was in the middle of a three-day detox with about twenty-five clients.

"Mom," she began before surprising me with an unusual request: "Can I do your detox program too?"

Together, we both ate everything on the detox plan for three days—veggies, beans, fish, lentils, avocado, nuts, and salads. No sugar, no caffeine, no meat and no grains. I didn't want to make a big deal of her decision or the meals I made for her, so we didn't talk much about it. Yet inside, I imagined giving her a big hug and high five. I was so proud to see that she wanted to nourish and nurture her body with healthy food as much as I did. We were connected in that.

That was how it started. Now, whenever Natalie is home, she enjoys trying my recipes, experimental meals and dinners, new combinations, whatever I'm making. The fact that she arrived at the conclusion to eat this way on her own, by listening to how different foods made her body feel good inside, was the most exciting and gratifying part of all. We took our own paths and arrived at the same rewarding conclusion. It's the only way I would have had it.

Now, we, Kelly, Scott, Natalie, and I, all eat the same food, and it feels like another milestone for us as a family, as a cohesive unit. I love having Natalie on my team.

14

keeping the balance

"Believe in your dreams and they will come true."

Kelly was able to comprehend and accept that my going to work was about helping others and teaching them the principles we'd been applying to our own bodies. This realization was effortless for her. It was a sign of how far we'd come, an indicator of how she continued to benefit from and embrace our lifestyle. She liked the idea of spreading the message, getting more people on our team.

Whenever I left the house for an evening client appointment and said, "I have to go to work." Kelly would respond with "Okay, Mom, have a good work."

While I was loving my new career coaching others, I kept an ever mindful eye on Kelly's IV treatments, supplements, and diet. I made sure that every day she had a fresh breakfast, lunch packed, and dinner ready as soon as she got home from school. I scheduled clients around Kelly's routine so I could be home with her every day after school.

Keeping the balance between work and home got more challenging around five to six weeks after Kelly's IV treatments, when the benefits started to wear off. I noticed it and so did Kelly.

"Mom, I feel foggy. I can't think. Can I get an IV?" Kelly had her own barometer. She felt it in her body and with challenges at school. Dark circles settled in under her eyes and her cheeks lost their rosy palette.

Epigenetic testing with Dr. Kane revealed that Kelly had a fatty acid metabolic disorder. She could not easily make her own phospholipids to support her cell membranes. That explained why she responded so beautifully and quickly to the fatty acid protocol and why she needed regular treatments every four to six weeks.

It was like the IV treatments were waking Kelly up to everything. She was more alert, more energetic, and more aware. Naturally, an awareness of being different started to become increasingly obvious to Kelly. For the first time, she started asking insightful, perceptive questions like why school was so difficult for her and why she had a hard time making or playing with friends. At times, she was angry about it. She blamed us and asked why there were so many things we'd never taught her, like how she couldn't do math and how spelling was so hard.

It became clear to us that we'd reached a juncture. Scott and I agreed that it was time to tell Kelly about autism. My hope was that it would help her understand her own challenges, and work through them. Rebecca, our behavior specialist at the time, who worked with Kelly two hours a week, agreed. She and I discussed the best way to tell Kelly without simply giving her a label. I did not want Kelly to blame autism for her unique differences, or use it as an excuse. She had come too far for that.

To help me characterize autism in the simplest, most relatable language, I bought a book called *The Autism Acceptance Book*, by Ellen Sabin. The book was typically used as a teaching tool for peers of students with autism. The perspective it offered was perfect for how I wanted to approach this delicate conversation with Kelly.

After I'd prepared myself by reading the book several times, I picked my date, the day I'd tell her. That sunny fall afternoon, Kelly and I went for a walk at a nearby park with a winding trail next to a stream—something we usually enjoyed doing on Sunday afternoons. Drawing on points from the book, I began to share with Kelly things I noticed about her. Slowly and in a curious tone, I stated what I'd observed in her.

"You have really good hearing, Kelly, and you also notice amazing details in things. But sometimes it's hard for you to understand what's happening around you or what people are saying." And I'd pause.

With each challenge, I'd give Kelly time to agree or disagree. I kept it simple and to the point. In the past, I would have been much more apprehensive to engage in this kind of conversation, a dialogue where intuitive probing questions peeled back the layers and allowed the other person to arrive at their own conclusions. It took some practice, but I had Integrative Nutrition to thank for my ability to approach it in this more enlightening and empowering way.

"Kelly," I continued, "there's something called autism. People with autism are like that. Because they hear so well, loud noises really bother them. Because they see the tiniest details, sometimes, things or faces look scary. Usually school is harder for them, and they often struggle to have friends." I paused.

Kelly nodded her head, saying, "Yeah, Mom, that's me."

As we strolled slowly by the stream, listening to the water trickle along, we talked through other strong traits of hers and the challenges she faced. Kelly asked questions about her personality, her friends, her diet, and school. She was curious why she'd missed so much, and she wanted to know how we'd work to get caught up. I was so impressed by her questions because they were the same ones I'd had for so long. In response, I told her simple, easy-to-understand highlights of everything I'd learned, everything pertinent I'd read over the years. I told her that, through it all, she had been my greatest teacher.

Luckily, Kelly embraced the idea of autism pretty quickly. It explained so much and gave her a name for why she was different, for the struggle. At this point, we'd already tackled a great deal, so presenting this diagnosis or label was only a small hurdle, and one I was grateful she could so easily overcome.

In the fall of 2011, two years after I started working with clients, we were faced with another big transition—Kelly would be entering high school. Montessori graduated students at the end of eighth grade, which meant that Kelly needed a new placement for high school.

Over the summer, with more psychological testing and meetings with our public school district, we argued that Kelly needed programming beyond what they could offer. Our position was backed by specific test scores and multiple recommendations from outside experts in the fields of neuropsychology, occupational therapy, and speech.

For example, the speech therapist who evaluated Kelly stated this in her report:

> *Due to Kelly's moderate to severe language processing disorder and pragmatic language disorder, she will require global adaptations to her day—familial, academic, and social. It will be important for her to socialize and learn in all academic environments that provide not only instructional support but also peers that have similar needs and interests.*

But before our public school district would agree to place Kelly somewhere other than their own program, we had to give their suggestions a chance.

One week before the school year started, the special education director presented their individualized placement for Kelly. It involved one-on-one instruction most of the day. Kelly's only mainstream class was art.

In art class, with zero accommodations, Kelly had no idea

what the teacher was talking about. She struggled to follow along and felt lost physically and emotionally. With that, and other uncomfortable experiences in the cafeteria and in social skills class, Kelly would come home confused, flustered and on the verge of tears. She desperately wanted to fit in but felt forced into an environment that simply wasn't appropriate for her functioning and cognitive ability. After about four weeks, the district agreed that Kelly's needs would be better met somewhere else.

One month into ninth grade, Kelly started at the Vanguard School—a publicly approved private school for special education that focused on integrated academic, social, and daily living skills in a supportive environment.

During the hour-long bus ride home after her first day, Kelly texted Scott in a panic: "Dad, is it okay for me to give out my phone number? Kids are asking me for it. I've never had anyone ask to be my friend before. What should I do?"

When Scott told me of the text exchange, I was shocked and thrilled. We both were. His long arms wrapped around my waist and squeezed me tight. As we embraced each other, we shared the joy of Kelly finding her place—a place where she could both make friends and learn.

Later that week, Kelly wrote a letter to the superintendent of our public school, thanking him for supporting her placement at Vanguard.

"Thank you for sending me to Vanguard," she wrote. "I'm so happy there and am finally learning." We'd never seen her so excited about school. Her entire body vibrated with happy, grateful energy.

A few days later, Kelly said, "Mom, this is so great. We should have a party! I actually learned today! The people are so friendly and they understand me. I love Vanguard!" She knew it instantly. It was the gift we'd been waiting for, the one that she deserved. She fit in.

15

live in love

"Let your love be stronger than your fear."

In mid-April of 2012, out of the blue, I got a phone call from one of my mentors and coaches, Stacy Morgenstern. She and her business partner, Carey Peters, wanted me to give an opening introduction for their upcoming live event, Holistic MBA or HMBA.

Over five hundred people, including some of my closest health coaching friends, would be at the event, all eager to learn more about coaching skills and manifesting big shifts in self-expression and financial freedom. My introduction would help kick off the event on May 2, 2012, in Tarrytown, New York.

At the time, Natalie was about to graduate from high school, and Kelly was finishing her first year at Vanguard. In the three years I'd been a health coach, I'd empowered a countless number of clients to embrace healthier lifestyles with great results. They were living pain-free, alleviating symptoms through dietary changes, and getting the support they needed to stick to it. I loved my new career, the girls were thriving in school, and life seemed good.

Everything was moving in a positive direction, all except for my dad's declining health condition. After battling flu-like symptoms for several months, in the beginning of April, he was diagnosed with MDS.

MDS, in so many words, is cancer. The doctor at South Miami

Hospital, where my dad was diagnosed, recommended blood trans-fusions at least once a week and prescribed Neupogen to boost my dad's blood counts. At this stage, my dad's body couldn't make any new blood cells on its own. Both the Neupogen and the transfusions masked a massive infection brewing in his body.

On Thursday, April 26, my dad was flown from Miami to Mass General Hospital in Boston, where they were experts on MDS. That same day, I drove from our home in Pennsylvania to Boston to be with him. The last time I'd seen my dad was the previous summer in Nantucket when he looked frail but still seemed in good health, despite his uphill struggle with Parkinson's disease.

The oncologists at Mass General told my parents that the only course of treatment was chemotherapy twice a week and blood transfusions weekly for the rest of my dad's life. To complicate matters, the treatment would have to be done at Mass General. This left my parents little choice but to move to Boston.

I spent the next four days with my dad. The first two were disturbingly rough because of the high doses of antibiotics and morphine running through his veins. The morphine made him delirious, irrational, and frighteningly paranoid. In the middle of the night, he called the hotel where my mom and I were sleeping. Panicked, he pleaded with my mom to come to the hospital and rescue him: "They are coming to get me. Help me, Marcia." It was two a.m.

The next day while I was alone with him in his hospital room, he got really ornery about the blinds on the window. He didn't like the way they were positioned and snapped at me over and over to fix them until all the blinds were perfectly lined up in straight rows. Kelly had trained me well for this sort of seemingly irrational sensory disturbance. I was perfectly suited to deal with him at this point and relieved my mom for most of the day.

On Saturday, the third day, my dad seemed to brighten up and had bursts of renewed, positive energy. He and I strolled down the hallway outside his room, his hands wrapped around the cold metal handle of his walker as his slippered feet shuffled on the shiny linoleum floor. I walked next to him at whatever pace he dictated. The nurses watched, admiring his determination. When he teased one of them, asking her to waltz with him, his eyes had a mischievous twinkle—the one I knew all so well.

That was my dad—always the charmer, never wanting to succumb to pain or negativity. "Mind over matter" and "No pain, no gain" were mottos he lived by. Growing up, he always preached to me and my sisters, "It's not what happens to you that matters. What matters most is how you react to it."

After our walk, when he was back in his hospital bed, he looked at me and shared the frustration of not being able to control his body or to slow down the aging process.

"This sucks," he said, forcing a half smile to break the mood. Then he went on: "I'm sorry I never followed your eating plan, Suzie." His regretful apology left me speechless. I reached for his hand and gently squeezed it.

On the last day I was there, Sunday, April 29, we were alone together in his hospital room. Barely able to move his arm, he surrendered to having me feed him turkey and mashed potatoes while he watched a baseball game on television.

My mind flashed back to when I was twelve years old and on vacation at our ski house in Stowe, Vermont. After a full day of skiing, my dad was sitting in the den all by himself, watching a football game and drinking a beer. With five daughters, he didn't often have companions when it came to sports games on television.

"Hi Dad," I said, walking in and sitting on the couch across from him, thinking I'd keep him company. The fire he'd made crackled in the background of the whistles blowing and commentators talking on the television.

His eyes fixated on the television as we sat alone together. I tried getting his attention by asking him to teach me how the game worked, specifically the "downs," which I'd never really understood. He explained the yards needed for a first down and other intricacies I hadn't realized about the game of football. Even if it was just football, it was a rare moment of teaching and bonding between him and I.

Now, thirty-five years later, we were sitting side-by-side again, alone together in his hospital room, watching baseball. Before leaving my dad on that Sunday night, I kissed the bare skin of his head and whispered, "Bye, Dad, I love you."

Right as the words left my mouth, his eyes closed. He'd succumbed to sleep without giving me any sign that he'd even heard me. He was weak and helpless, the roomy hospital gown hanging off his pale, bony figure. Barely able to move, pain pulsated through his body relentlessly. The only comfort I had was in knowing that he was starting chemo the following day and that I'd be back to see him again in a week.

That night, I drove from Boston back home to our house in Pennsylvania. With two days to spare, I'd unpack, regroup, do laundry, stock the fridge, and repack before leaving again to attend the HMBA event which started on Wednesday, May 2. Needless to say, I hardly had time to process what was happening.

Early Wednesday morning, I arrived in Tarrytown, New York. Excited to connect with the other coaches I'd been in a mastermind group with for the past year, I settled into the hotel room I was sharing with one of them. We hadn't seen each other since our retreat in Phoenix six months earlier.

Later that day, when it was time for the event to kick off, I was told to stand in one corner of the large conference room facing the crowd. Across the room from me, in the opposite corner with a metal microphone stand positioned in front of her, was another coach and friend of mine from the mastermind group. The two of us had been chosen to give the introduction. Beforehand, she'd rehearsed the speech she prepared with me. Meanwhile, I'd barely had time to plan my delivery or memorize a single word. As an involuntary rush of nerves crashed over me, I clenched my notes—a crumpled piece of paper with scribbles—tightly in my hand.

Suddenly and unexpectedly, the room turned dark. Then, bam, a blinding bright spotlight flipped on, centering right at my face. I was not prepared for this. I looked out at all the people, sitting there, waiting for me to speak some memorable, inspirational words of wisdom.

My throat closed with panic. I bent over to get closer to the microphone, but I couldn't speak. *If I can't see my notes, what will I say?* I was naked without them. I'd never spoken about something I felt so passionately about in front of a crowd this large. I was so focused on not messing it up, I was paralyzed. *Say something! Get it together,* my brain pounded back at me, a rally cry. Finally, I blurted out some nonsense about how successful my health coaching practice was and how much I loved Carey and Stacy, the coaches I was introducing.

They'd chosen me for a reason, and I felt like I was letting them down. Ironically, everything they'd been teaching and mentoring me to become was about stepping into my spotlight, owning my message, and being a beacon for change. I imagined I'd shrunken into a tiny nothing, unnoticeable, and unable to make an impact on anyone.

Forgiveness was not on my mind, only disappointment, guilt, and shame. I was being too hard on myself, I know, but I was emotionally fragile. In the days before, I'd been watching my father's body slowly shut down on him. I'd had to help him eat, walk, and hold a plastic container for him so he could urinate without leaving his bed. *How could I possibly accept that this was nearing the end?*

Once I found my seat and began slowly breathing deep breaths, I realized the truth was that it wasn't what I uttered in that panicked moment that bothered me. That was all true. And it was only a moment, a few sentences. What upset me was how I'd said it—my voice was void of passion and showed a lack of confidence. The words were coming from a place of fear and desire to craft the perfect sentences, deliver a flawless presentation, and prove some sort of perceived level of accomplishment.

At first, it seemed I failed because I couldn't remember what I'd written down, but the bigger issue was that I didn't trust myself to just know what to say.

Later Wednesday night, when I was out to dinner in Tarrytown with friends from the event, I got the call.

"Dad's not doing well," said my oldest sister, Wini, breaking the news to me.

"Are you sure? How could that be?" I said in disbelief, trying to wrap my brain around the possibility that my dad was dying. "Three days ago, we sat, talked, and watched a baseball game together. Of course, he was in pain, but he was prepared for the next phase," I pleaded. She listened.

"The final bone biopsy results came back. There are no healthy blood cells left in his body, Suz." Slowly, Wini's resigned tone reported the bad news to me. Since she'd been with him in Florida and watched his deterioration over the past month, she'd come to accept the inevitable quicker than me. "The doctor isn't saying how much time he has left, but he's drifting in and out of consciousness."

I should go be with him. The daughter and sister in me felt incredible guilt for being at the HMBA event and not at the hospital.

Then, the grown up in me fought back. *I need to do this.* This was an important moment in standing up for who I've become—a person who, above all, loves and respects other people with a mission to encourage them to honor themselves. Listening to that foreign new voice inside my head, telling me to choose to honor this moment for myself and my career, I stayed in Tarrytown for the remaining two days of the event, knowing I could leave sooner if the news with my dad worsened.

"Okay, I'll keep you posted. Who knows? This could drag on for days or weeks," Wini reassured me, respecting my decision.

Immediately after hanging up, I called Scott to fill him in. I shared my plan to stay at the conference until Saturday, then drive straight to Boston to be with my dad instead of coming home.

"Do what you have to do, Suz," he said, letting me know he understood. He was fine to take care of Kelly while I was gone.

Then I spoke to Natalie who was away in Connecticut.

"No! Isn't there something they can do?" Natalie protested, sobbing.

"I know, I wish there was, but the doctors say it's too late," I responded, my voice cracking with tears.

"I want to see him," she softly begged, sniffling. She was in Connecticut without a car, I was in Tarrytown, New York, Scott was home with Kelly in Pennsylvania, and my dad was in Boston.

"Maybe this weekend," I offered not sure how we'd make it work.

On Saturday, the final day of the event, our mastermind group had a VIP exclusive lunch with Carey and Stacey. It would be the last time we'd all be together. I needed to say goodbye to my friends and mentors. As soon as lunch was over and several parting tears were shed, I got in my car and started driving. My mom and three of my sisters were already with my dad. Like me, my sister Beth was on her way there on a flight from Newark to Boston.

When I was about two hours away from the hospital, my cell phone rang. It was my sister, Wini.

"Suzie," she said through a shaky voice. "Dad just died."

My breath stopped, then I screamed, "No! No, no, no!" I told him I'd be back. I'd let him down.

I don't remember the car ride after that, but somehow I managed to drive despite the blinding, violent sobs. Trying to get there as fast as possible, I drove eighty mph. I was so mad that I missed seeing Dad one more time, so distraught and disappointed I wasn't there when he passed.

It was a full moon and Cinco de Mayo the day my dad died, Saturday, May 5, 2012. He was seventy-eight years old and his fiftieth wedding anniversary was just months away. When I got to the hospital, Wini and Lori, my two older sisters, met me at the entrance. They grabbed me hard, and we all hugged.

"Do you want to see him?" Wini asked, as if now that he was dead, I might not want to lay eyes on his waxing facial expression and rigid body.

"Yes," I blubbered, without hesitation or doubt. "Yes, of course I do. I have to see him." I didn't care what he looked like.

He was still in the same hospital bed where I'd left him Sunday night, just six days before. When I walked into the room, my body vibrated uncontrollably with the reality of death. He was gone.

Sadness came over me in a way it hadn't ever before in my life. It knocked the wind out of me, making my body convulse and my knees weak. I went and sat on the edge of the bed next to his legs. I placed one of my hands on his hand, the same sweaty hand that held mine on the day I got married. Underneath the hair on his skin, I felt warmth as if he was still there, still alive. Then, I placed my other hand on his leg as if to connect with him through touch, through the warm blood still in his body. I stayed there for maybe an hour, maybe longer. My sisters came and went, talking around me and out in the hall, but I wasn't ready to move. I didn't want to leave him.

His spirit was still in his body. I knew he felt me too. In that tender, out-of-body moment, the message was clear. It was okay that I hadn't been there sooner. He forgave me. He loved me. I felt a greater love than ever before. The moments we'd shared just days before were tender and loving. I'd cherish them forever.

The weeks that followed were some of the most difficult of my life. The grief was unbearable, and I'd indulge myself in it. I cried so many tears I didn't know I had any left to cry. Kelly comforted me in her own way, granting me time and space to grieve. She hugged me often to offer solace. I didn't have to explain. Somehow she just understood.

Exactly one month after my dad passed, the message in my daily meditation book, *Journey to the Heart,* by Melody Beattie, was this:

Believing in life means it's okay to let go.
We can trust where we've been.
We trust where we are going.
And we're right where we need to be now.
Believe in life.

The passage prompted me to see how, for a very long time, I'd been clinging to the past, to fear, to beliefs I'd been taught but didn't authentically believe. In that moment, reading the meditation, I decided I was ready to let go of the grief and loss—the loss of my father, the loss of expected hopes and dreams of what life would be like as a parent. I was ready to let them go and once I did, it sparked a conscious, deliberate shift in me. Above all else, I chose life. I chose love.

My dad's death permitted me to truly embrace letting go of fear and to consciously live in love once and for all. It comforted me to know my dad was with God, and warmed me to feel a love greater than I'd ever felt before from him, with him. It was a peaceful acceptance. His spirit was loving me in a way that my mortal father never could.

In those moments of epiphany I fully understood that love comes from God, or at least it does for me. I also very clearly saw that life was about how you make people feel, not what you do or accomplish.

At my dad's memorial service, two months after he died, I read a passage from Ecclesiastes. I stood up in front of over three hundred people, including his lifelong friend, Roger Penske, who would be giving his eulogy after my reading. My voice was loud and clear. "There is a time for everything and a season for every activity under the heavens . . . a time to be born and a time to die . . ."

My faith in my ability to be a powerful leader, advocating for what I believed in, was restored. I could speak to crowds. I just needed to know exactly what I was talking about—not the words, but the message. Most of all, I needed to lead with my heart, with love. I needed to trust that inner voice and always, always live in love.

16

be your own hero

"Life is awesome when you just know how to look on the bright side and have fun doing everything you do."

Almost exactly three years later, in late May of 2015, soon after Kelly's nineteenth birthday, I was standing over the laundry basket, folding clean clothes from the dryer, when Kelly came to find me. She asked me a question, and as I turned toward her to answer, the innocence and purity of her spirit poured out of her eyes, hypnotizing me. Kelly's intense inquisitive gaze put me in a trance, my eyes fixated on hers.

"When I look in your eyes, I see God," Kelly told me.

Eyes locked, we stood facing each other, our feet surrounded by dirty clothes, cat food, and shoes. I was frozen in time and space. My mind got quiet while her mesmerizing stare reminded me of all the things she'd taught me. Most of all, she taught me that what mattered wasn't crossing things off the to-do list, such as accomplishments, promotions, money made, or other measurements of success. Instead, what had meaning and impact, what was important to me, was how people feel when they are with you, because of you. I'd always wanted Kelly to feel love in spite of everything. I chose love and it worked.

Like a magnet, her gaze glued to mine, I understood that Kelly could transform a moment, shift perspective with a look, radiate love and light—all through her eyes and her smile. It was pure magic. Hers was an expression void of agenda, history, or baggage. Instead, it represented contagious, peaceful happiness, a boomerang of love. Perfect karma—what goes around comes around.

"I love Kelly's smile," the nurse said one day after she put the catheter in Kelly's arm for her IV treatment. "It's contagious."

Until that moment, I didn't realize how Kelly was able to impact people, other than just me, with her smile. The way her lips spontaneously form a soft, virtuous grin spreads feelings of love, acceptance, and happiness. Kelly's innocent spirit is a beacon of love and light with the power to bring meditative pause to any situation.

Even though Kelly said she witnessed God in my eyes, I believe it's love that she saw—deep, unconditional love and compassion for all she'd been through, all we'd been through. But perhaps she could also feel a connection beyond the two of us, a force or power greater than us that was rooted in love. It's the bright side.

Years of self-exploration in therapy, journaling, and dietary changes all contributed to the shift in my perspective. Even though I had many *aha* moments along the way, it wasn't a switch that flipped instantaneously. But then, unexpectedly and unwaveringly, I reached a place where I felt the energy of being connected to something much bigger than me, my family, or anyone around me.

It took cleaning up my diet, focusing on real food, uniting our family with that approach, joining the Integrative Nutrition community, and using the mirror of loving my clients that all positively and profoundly culminated my transformation.

Scott's unconditional love and support gave me the confidence and security I needed to power through the rough times. His support was my springboard, the energy that empowered me to embark on the journey of self-growth and stick to it. None of this would have been possible without his loyal commitment to me and to our family, to what we were building together.

"Thank you for loving me," I'll say, reminding him often of my profound gratitude. He knows what that love has made possible for us and our family.

After shifting my body and mindset with the consistent, committed journey of healing with love and food, I'm able to give myself little gifts of kindness every day. It's not perfect or constant, but it's a non-negotiable mindfulness. Now, I focus on loving myself by pampering my body with real, nourishing, delicious homemade food, and exercise such as walking or strengthening my muscles with resistance or other training—not out of punishment or obligation, but out of love and honor.

By surrendering to just loving Kelly, I realized that the things she had trouble with or couldn't do didn't matter anymore. The fact that she was different became insignificant. Rather, it became beautiful and brilliant. Instead of focusing my energy on correcting, teaching, or changing things, I found peace in appreciating every little good thing and, of course, the big things, too—like her ability to develop empathy for others. Empathy is not something that people with autism usually feel or develop. Remarkably, Kelly has learned to understand other people's feelings.

"Mom, how was your day?" Kelly curiously inquires after she shares hers with me. One night, after reluctantly voicing some of my frustration to her, Kelly adamantly professed, "Mom, I like when you tell me how you're feeling. It goes both ways you know." She said it all in those few, simple words. I may be her mom, she would always be my daughter, but we could be equal in so many things and lean, hard, on one another. *It goes both ways, now I know.*

In the past few years, with her growing self-esteem at Vanguard, Kelly has begun expressing her gratitude for the small stuff like the dinner I make for her or the time we spend together talking after school, but the appreciation goes deeper than just the moment. It is rooted in her understanding of the journey.

Every day she says, "Thanks for dinner, Mom," "I love you, Mom," and "Dad, you and me are so lucky to have Mom." Her gratitude feeds my soul, keeps me going, grounds me in love.

It had been fourteen years since we sat in Dr. Altman's office and found out Kelly had PDD, or autism. In those grueling years, we'd been chasing hope and finding it in only small doses here and there. Now, we are finally in a place where Kelly's spirit is able to shine. It shows through the sparkle in her eyes and in the way her smile oozes with an effortless, affectionate energy of acceptance, innocence, and comfortable confidence. Her unpredictable, easily agitated fog is now a distant memory. Kelly is finally Kelly.

Kelly was, and continues to be, a beautiful spirit who, maybe, needed more love and attention than other children her age, but that was okay as long as I let go of expectations and just loved her. Thankfully, she felt that never-ending, authentic, pure love. Kelly taught me that she is precious because of her spirit, who she is on the inside, not because of what she does. I believe that is true of any child or human being.

But for Kelly, there was no celebration of accomplishments in measurable form like grades, test scores, soccer goals, or other tangible victories. Because she'd never been a part of that world, she didn't compare herself to others. I learned from her that acceptance is the ultimate form of love.

Growing up in my family, there was a sense of unspoken competition to go faster, be better, and mingle with the right people to prove something. We were taught to be good and to do good, not that we were innately good. With this model, a common one for many families of our generation, we ended up feeling like we were never good enough. The attachment to external feedback and results made me want to control, and then I had a hard time giving up control because I relied on it like a thermometer, clock, or scale.

So in comparing and striving to be like others, which I did for years, I lost my own internal power and acumen. By giving it away to those external measurements and standards like I did, based on my family's culture, I lost touch with my true self. When

I sacrificed my innate, loving intuition and my inner wisdom and strength, I became attached to fear. Living in fear only led to anxiety and entrapment.

On the contrary, relying on my inner wisdom and love led to peace and freedom. Journeying with Kelly, surrendering to love, and letting go of expectation and fear gave me that gift.

Kelly taught me that love is more than a feeling, it's energy—an energy that extends way beyond ourselves, far outside our bodies and the space we occupy. It connects us to a higher power, a divine light. That's what Kelly sees when she looks into my eyes, but it wasn't always there. I had to find it within myself. It was hidden deep down inside.

For me, living in love is the ultimate priority, the only way to be. In order to trust it, though, I needed to experience this magic, this unconditional love for myself. Kelly helped me do that.

Kelly feels her spirit sparkle and knows that she can channel a power higher than herself, but it overwhelms her sometimes. Lately, instead of keeping it inside and letting it frustrate her, Kelly shares her thoughts and feelings with me, trying to process and understand them. Her newfound clarity, through Dr. Kane's treatments, empowers her to feel grounded in faith. It speaks to her.

One day, sitting at the kitchen counter, doing her homework, Kelly looked over at me.

"You know, Mom, I can feel a spirit when I'm near one. Like at JoJo's memorial service, I could tell he was standing there. Is that crazy, Mom?"

I told her to go on. I wanted to know more. Then she jumped to a different example, perhaps less scary to her.

"Like Dr. Kane. She has a fully good spirit. I can feel it," Kelly continued.

"Maybe it's because she loves you and understands you so well," I said, offering some possible clarity.

"No, Mom. Not just love. Love's an intention that comes from the heart. Spirit is another thing. Spirit is deep inside everybody even though they are not aware of it."

The pure love and spirit emanating from Kelly melts away fear and the inclination to compare and despair.

"I don't know why people compare themselves to others. They should just be happy with who they are," Kelly declared one day when frustrated with a friend who was unhappy after she compared herself to someone else. "I hate when people do that!"

Kelly can walk into a room and not be worried about what her hair looks like, whether she's wearing makeup (which she rarely does), or what clothes she's chosen. Instead, standing and breathing confidence, she notices the details of the room—the light, the color, the decorations, and most of all, the energy. She generously compliments others, sharing the light, spreading the love.

There are little reminders of the energy of the universe, of love, that show up in all kinds of ways—in the birds that fly around us, in the tree branches and leaves that dance in the breeze, and in the benevolent, spontaneous smile of a stranger. It's there waiting for us to discover.

Years ago, I would have pointed the finger at autism, blaming it for our tornado of bad days, sickness, erratic behaviors, sleepless nights, dips in my own health, and stresses on the family to name just a few. Today, I'm so grateful for the lessons it's forced us to learn. Having autism in our family initiated the process of showing me how to surrender to loving in an unconditional way. Giving myself permission to experience the loss opened up space for me to feel the love. Getting past fear and discovering the deepest place inside of me where the love lives: that's when all the magic started to happen.

In the core of being: there's a whole new world that lights up because of the surrender. The more I stepped into love, the more love came back to me. I told myself to focus on love over and over again. I reminded myself until one day, it became easier and joy flowed effortlessly through me. Every bird's fluttering wings and every smile that sparkled radiated more joy, more love. The amazing part is that once you get there, once you are living in love, every situation you enter into brings you to that Zen place where miracles happen.

When I stand naked in front of the mirror and look long enough to see past the wrinkles, crooked bones, and bumpy cellulite, I can find the inner beauty reflected in my flaws—those perfect imperfections. Focusing on within, I crave time to visit and nurture my soul and enjoy my quiet, meditative morning time where I write to release all the swirling thoughts in my head.

What I'm talking about is not just a shift inside of us. Yes, that's where it begins and where we feel its power, but eventually, that energy can affect everything around us. It can change how we perceive our world, how those in our world perceive us.

Suddenly, the partner or husband who never takes the garbage out can be easily forgiven. You can drop the resentment that you're the one getting out of bed to get the kids ready for school, and trust that inputs and outputs are balanced. Instead of pushing them away, you can begin to long for their kiss, their touch, or an intimate conversation. Before we know it, they are taking out the garbage, asking how they can help, and giving us permission to lean on them. It takes both effort and a leap of faith, which I remind my clients about all the time, but eventually they see it working. That change starts inside. It starts inside you.

I'll still forget every now and then that there are going to be rough days that are far from perfect. I'll slip and beat myself up over something small that, in the moment, seems huge—like dropping my cell phone in the toilet, burning dinner, or being emotionally rattled by someone with road rage yelling at me for being in their way. Then, I breathe. Kelly reminds me to breathe. Natalie texts me, and I remember she's on our team. Scott walks through the door with his loving grin, reminding me that we still share that same, fiery love we did years ago as teenagers.

I look in the mirror at the end of these days, and I say: *I love and appreciate you. I love that you're committed, authentic, and loyal. I love how your wrinkles express the grueling, long journey from where you started to where you are now. I love your body just as it is. I love your unique way of seeing things. I love that you're sensitive and feel the energy around your own body and self. I love the food you eat and how you choose nourishing yourself above all else. I love the way you love others. I love living in this magical way of connecting through love to the universe.*

Often, parents of children with autism focus on healing their child, sometimes at any cost. We did that too, absolutely, but in the process, what happened was that Kelly healed me. I don't believe I ever could have realized this kind of healing without her as my guiding light.

"On the bright side" became one of Kelly's customary phrases. I don't remember the day it started or why, but somehow she found a way to see things in that light. Daily, she reflects on a situation from her day and presents a glass-half-full perspective. Kelly is able to find the bright side in every situation. "On the bright side, it's a sunny day," she says after sharing a difficult situation that happened at school, or "Even though I didn't get the part I wanted in the play, on the bright side, it will be fun to be in it."

Kelly is finding her way on her own and also with our help. We are so lucky. She's become her own hero with me, Scott, and Natalie by her side, cheering her on. Our support may continue to be necessary moving forward as she finds her own path beyond Vanguard, but her foundation is strong.

Kelly, without knowing it, taught me that in nurturing the body, we also nurture our spirit. Often, we look to the outside for answers, guidance, and healing. But the answer is on the inside, hidden from our view and thoughts. So it's easy to forget that it's there. Yet, it waits patiently for us to connect and to trust its guiding light. We search books, enroll in programs, consult with therapists, and confide in friends. While they may guide us, we need to nurture and nourish our body with our own love, honoring that spirit within. Your inner spirit is what will keep you grounded, centered, balanced, and focused on your passion and purpose.

One day, I was taking a walk outside when my sister, Wini, called me about a situation with one of her three teenage boys.

"What is it all about anyway? What's the point?" she quizzically protested in mutiny of motherhood.

I tried offering some sort of solace: "I think it's about what's inside of us, about our relationship with ourselves. That's where we find the love to understand and accept everything else. Maybe that's what we are working toward. After all, it's what we are left with in the end."

The only thing that matters, the only thing that is real in any given moment is love. It's more than an emotion, more than an intentional action, as Kelly taught me. It's a compass for our relationships, with ourselves and with others, whether they're fleeting or for a lifetime.

Before she moved to Nashville, Taylor Swift lived a block away from our house. When she was around four or five years old, her mom and I were on the same committee for the Junior League of Reading. It was a fundraiser called Whale of a Sale—a huge yard sale outside at a picnic ground. During set-up, in the numerous pavilions where merchandise was being sorted, priced, and displayed, Taylor pranced around in her brown leather cowboy boots, pink skirt, adorable smile, and long blonde ringlets. I remember being in awe of the way her spirit soared free as she danced around all of us with her own rhythm.

In July of 2015, Scott got tickets to Taylor's *1989* concert at MetLife Stadium where he grew up going to Giants games with his dad. It was a beautiful, sunny summer Friday afternoon with a light, refreshing New York breeze. Named after Taylor's birth year, *1989* is about self-discovery. The crowd roared to its feet with her opening song, "Welcome to New York."

I danced, screamed, and sang alongside Kelly, Natalie, and Scott while crying tender tears of joy. I cried for Taylor, for her story and her overwhelming success. I cried for us, tears of celebration, and relief. We'd finally made it. Everything we'd done was working, finally working. Yes, it was finally working. And it was totally worth it. For days after the concert, tears continued to spill out of my eyes whenever I revisited that moment with my girls and Scott, listening to Taylor's voice reverberate through the stadium.

The next time we were together again as a family was a few weeks later, in the same spot we revisited every summer since Natalie was born—Surfside Beach, Nantucket. It was the beach where Scott and I spent many googly-eyed nights gazing up at stars as teenagers. Now, Natalie and Kelly lay in the sand behind us on their blue-and-white-striped beach towels, each with a book in hand. Scott and I sat next to each other in beach chairs, staring out at the ocean, lost in thought and conversation. All of our hands reached into the cooler at one time or another to share strawberries, nuts, nutrient-dense gluten-free pretzels, hummus, and chicken.

I pondered—maybe life's wonder was about the unpredictable, uncontrollable stuff. Maybe that's what it's all about instead of what we imagine it to be or think we can create.

The gentle sway of ocean ripples sparkling from the sun gave me the same feeling as looking into Kelly's eyes—deep blue, mysterious beauty. Peace, love, understanding, and connection. A seal popped his head out of the water, pausing to stare at our family as if inviting us in to play. The ocean waves crashed gently on the sand in a relaxing rhythmic sound that allowed minutes and hours to pass without noticing.

Natalie asked Kelly if she wanted to go swimming. In their bikinis, they got up and walked down to the ocean's edge. After a brief moment of reflection and respect, the two sisters ran in the water and dove into an approaching wave, right at that sweet spot before the wave crashed. Together, we'd all found the bright side.

hope

Written by Kelly Carpenter, age ten

If you want hope, you can't just get hope. You really have to make hope. The world is not going to do it for you. You need to make it happen. It's not that hard. You can just tell yourself, do it.

Life has a lot of stuff. If you need anything, just reach for it. Anything is possible. You just have to have faith, trust, and courage. The change I want to see in the world is more trust and hope because it's what we need more of.

Why? Because a lot of people I see and know are really sad and I want to change that. People have the power to turn their cheek and that means to move on because that's part of life and people forget that. I don't like people being sad so I want to help make it better.

You just have to try your best and that's all you can do.

I'm kind of sad about how I got really sick and finding out I had food allergies. I felt really sad and hurt when it happened. But I moved on and now I'm happier and can eat a lot of stuff because I really believed I could get better and did.

afterword

People tell me all the time that I "saved" Kelly, but that's not completely true. I hesitate to take the credit. It was her journey as much as it was mine. Side-by-side, breathing the same air, we climbed the mountain together.

Along the way, our stamina and endurance depended on Scott and Natalie's support. We needed their stability, their foundation at the foot of the mountain, while the two of us set up, hiking toward the summit. It took us fifteen years to get to the top. But we did it. Now, we stand hand-in-hand on the rocky peak, appreciating a magnificent view, the bright side.

While writing this memoir, I dug up old journals from those early years—the years when Kelly was younger and sick, when I was still sick. Up high on the top shelf of a storage closet in our house, there must have been twenty or more spiral notebooks stashed in a cardboard box along with all the doctors' notes, bills, test results, and emails.

I thought I remembered how confusing things were during those dark days, but as I read the words, the inked messages my own hand put down on paper, I was shocked. The intense daily grind came pounding back. I could feel the frustration, impatience, and resentment in my words, often misdirected at Scott, myself, or the uncontrollable nature of our situation. Because I was sick, I couldn't see clearly.

Rereading those reflections in my journal writing, though difficult to get through at times, offered me the chance to appreciate our journey with a new perspective. The process has left me in awe of where we've been and where we've landed. The frustration, fear, and pain I felt in the years that Kelly was ill and in an irritable fog has now transformed into a blessing. With the clear skies that came from healing, I could finally see the light and breathe in gratitude for the journey.

Scott and Natalie's roles were just as important as mine and Kelly's. Though it was a sort of unspoken agreement, we all knew that we needed to work together, each with his or her own critical part. Every single day, I feel gratitude for the partnership, the family rally around the crisis, and our incredible transformation.

Now that we are together, on the bright side, let me tell you a little bit more about Kelly and where she was at the time I sat down to write our story.

Kelly is a brave, beautiful, expressive nineteen-year-old woman. She is creative, spirited, determined, kind, and caring. Her life is simple but rich. When she's not in school at Vanguard, she's watching movies on her laptop, building and decorating houses on Sims, playing Let's Dance, shooting hoops, or riding her favorite horse, Sunny. Her pace is slower, more methodical than the rest of the family (there's no rushing Kelly), but the fact that she lives in the moment grounds her.

On New Year's Eve, December 31, 2014, I asked everyone at our dining room table to choose a word of the year, a word that would be their guiding light for 365 days, a powerful compass. Just one word, that's it. Kelly chose "independence." True to her word and determination, this past year, 2015, has been all about independence for Kelly.

In March of 2015, Kelly passed her driver's license permit test on her first try—an accomplishment that transformed her perspective of herself and her limitless potential. This simple piece of paper, a rite of passage for most teenagers across the country, was a key milestone for Kelly. Though she may have had to study much harder than they did, making flash cards and memorizing the rules over and over, despite the challenge, it reminded her that she can do anything she puts her mind to. We believed this about her all along, but more and more she is discovering it for herself.

At her high school graduation in June of 2015, as vice president of her class, Kelly gave the welcome address to the audience and her classmates. Honored, Kelly stood in front of the audience, smiled, and confidently spoke a warm greeting. She'd made it through many ups and downs in a variety of schools, but finally spent four years at one that was a fit for her where she'd made friends and learned like never before. She was proud. We were proud.

Even though she'd completed high school, Kelly would stay at the Vanguard School for another two years. In the fall of 2015, Kelly started the transition program at Vanguard, which included going to a job at a retail store with a job coach two days a week and continuing to further her practical math and reading skills the other three days a week.

About a month into the 2015 school year, one of her teachers commented on Kelly's emerging confidence. Instead of sweatshirts and jeans every day, Kelly wears nice blouses, skirts, and dresses to school. She talks to a wide range of students, offering advice to them, and still has a strong curiosity to learn, openly asking questions and seeking knowledge on a variety of topics.

In October, Kelly decided she wanted to audition for the Vanguard school play, which she'd had only a minor role in the year before—her first play ever. Knowing the competition would be stiff, in the weeks leading up to tryouts, Kelly practiced lines every single day, memorizing them and the song, "Part of My World." On the night before tryouts, Kelly couldn't sleep because she was so excited. Then, the next day, Kelly stood on stage by herself, without any prompting or script, and acted out the requested scene and song without a blip. Under pressure, she shined.

"Mom, it was just like what I did when I was little, pretending to be the characters in movies. I only stopped acting like that because I was afraid of what other people might think. But now it feels really good to do it again."

Kelly's energy on stage, the way she dramatically waved her arms and changed her facial expressions along with the tone of her voice to show the emotion of the scene, elevated her performance. The two weeks of practicing, memorizing lines, searching for examples on YouTube, and singing her heart out paid off. Kelly got the lead role, Ariel, in *The Little Mermaid*.

At the end of 2015, we hosted Thanksgiving at our house for the first time in ten years. With twenty-four people coming, Kelly worried she would be overwhelmed by the amount of activity and the noise from buzzing conversations. I told her she could stay in her room as long as she needed to.

But she didn't run off to hide in her room. Instead, she went to the park and played football with her cousins and then chatted with their girlfriends and wives in our kitchen before dinner. In the middle of the gathering, Kelly pulled me aside and said, "Mom, I'm so grateful to be part of this family. Is it okay if I tell everyone that?"

Autism is only part of a person, and its only part of our story. Kelly was *Kelly* first—a fragile young girl with feelings, trying to express herself. She had something to say and we needed to hear her.

The rest of the story is about love, about mothers and daughters, about learning to trust and let go of expectations, about finding a Zen place. It's about trusting your gut and staying true to your values, even when you're in doubt and in despair and feeling like you're against all odds.

It's a story that can apply to all of us, a story that can turn out surprisingly celebratory in the end. Look, we're living proof that even in the midst of uncontrollable chaos, determination and unconditional love will prevail. Love must come first.

Today I have a daily practice that's meditative in nature where I wake up every morning before anyone else. My iPad plays soft, relaxing music while I visit with myself, writing, breathing, thinking, appreciating. For forty-five minutes, I relish in this peaceful, reflective space where my undivided attention goes to listening to my body and heart.

When I look at the journal entries I'm writing today, they are vastly different from those of years ago. Rather than clearly written notes documenting events, now my words on paper are a scribbled symphony that describe and celebrate Kelly's new independence, her determination, stamina, kindness, and refreshing approach to life. Those scribbles discuss the inspiration I feel from her bright side mentality and positive outlook. Instead of a struggle to record, my pen moves quickly across the paper, overflowing with gratitude for lessons *learned*.

Every day during my journaling, I remind myself of how important it is that I continue to endure the daily climb of making every meal from scratch and always loving Kelly unconditionally, setting aside time to listen to her after school for an hour or more while she shares her day, vents, and processes. I write about Kelly's excitement over new delicious recipes like whoopee pies, meatball subs, or grilled marinated Denver steak. My words relish in Kelly's prophetic insights on life, reminders of her unique and brilliant spirit that was never measured in IQ or other psychological testing.

As part of her intention to be more independent in 2015, Kelly began her own practice of journaling so she could process, make sense of, and release her feelings. For so many years, she'd been leaning on me to be her sounding board and while she still does, she learned that journaling gives her a sense of freedom to explore her emotions in a new way. As she writes, she develops a better understanding of events that happened, or how she wants to feel, and shifts her perspective.

Recently one night, I walked into her room while she was journaling about a difficult day that had her in tears moments before. Our eyes met and I told her how much I loved her, how amazing I thought she was. Still staring into my eyes, she beamed and proudly affirmed herself: "I know, Mom. I am amazing. I love myself too."

acknowledgments

The odyssey between the idea of this book and finally seeing our story come together on paper was extraordinary. I'm so grateful for the help of Round Table Companies, specifically for my writing coach, Francesca. Francesca, I couldn't have pulled this all together without you. Your ever thoughtful encouragement and gentle guidance gave me the confidence I needed to keep writing, to find the right words so I could show, not tell, my story.

There are so many angels that gently held my hand and shined a light on my path during those times of darkness. It is remarkable to think of all the people on the journey, and I want to thank each and every one, even if I forget to mention names.

First and foremost, I need to thank my husband, Scott, for his unwavering love and support. For all the years he stood by lovingly and loyally while I was consumed with experimenting and directing Kelly's therapies, diet, and daily care. Scott, thank you for sticking by me. You are my number one, always.

To Natalie: thank you for enduring the battle by my side, being patient, helpful, kind, and also honest. I adore you.

To Kelly: thank you for allowing me to share our story. Thank you for always trusting me and accepting all the changes we implemented over the years. Your courage is an inspiration to so many.

I hope you will share your voice with the world.

To Patricia Kane: thank you for loving Kelly and for bringing out her light. No one understands her like you do and that has been one of the greatest gifts.

To my father, for always instilling the motto, "It's not what happens to you that matters most but how you react to it." I wish you could read this book, but I know you've been here with me, lovingly cheering me on.

To my mom, for rescuing me when I needed you most, for making me hamburgers for breakfast, for teaching me how to cook, and for continually bringing beauty and magic into our lives.

To all my sisters who are a circle of love, the foundation of my being: you are the most amazing aunts. Thank you for always listening.

To my intuitive coach and dear friend, Carrie Saba: thank you for stretching me and being my cheerleader with this book and everything I do.

To all my teachers, coaches, and healers: thank you for guiding me to believe in myself, to be true to my core values, to trust my inner wisdom, and to, above all else, love myself.

To my clients: thank you for teaching me things about myself I couldn't see without your mirror. Thank you for trusting me to be your partner in health and well-being.

To all the therapists and teachers who work tirelessly with children on the autistic spectrum to help them discover their unique magic, to feel heard and understood. It is here, in these safe spaces, where self-esteem is fostered and sparks are ignited.

To Bob and Suzanne Wright, for your loving determination to raise awareness for autism and give a voice to millions of people around the world.

And last but not least, I want to thank our toy poodle, Sofie, for the countless hours she laid by my side while I wrote this book.

As with many things, hopefully this is the not the end, but a new beginning. But first I will sit down, breathe several long deep breaths, pinch myself, and cry tender tears of joy.

Made in the USA
Middletown, DE
08 December 2016